TABLE OF CONTENTS

Introduction

"I vow to my fellow citizens, and to the friends who reside among us, that the State will be vigilant about their security and well-being. Our nation is capable, by the Grace of God Almighty and the unity of its citizens, to confront and destroy the threat posed by a deviant few and those who endorse or support them. With the help of God Almighty, we shall prevail."

Crown Prince Abdullah bin Abdulaziz[1]

There is a fundamental difficulty when defining what constitutes an Islamic extremist/terrorist. This problem arises from no universally recognized definition, as well as, the terms are usually defined through cultural viewpoint. Within the Kingdom of Saudi Arabia (hereafter, the Kingdom) an extremist, or jihadist, is typically defined as one who perverts the Islamic religion or conducts themselves contrary to the approved *Ulema* council, scholars that influence Islamic society, standards for behavior within the Kingdom.[2] The Union of the Moslem World developed a definition of terrorism that it would like the global community to accept. Their definition reads:

> Terrorism is the aggression practiced by individuals, groups or states oppressing human beings' religion, life, money and honor. It includes all forms of fear, hurt, threat, killing without right, banditry and all actions of violence and threatening committed by individuals or collectively aiming to frighten, hurt or risk people's lives. Also it includes environmental damage and destruction of public and private utilities. All these terrorist deeds are considered as mischief in the land and are prohibited by the Holy Quran.[3]

This definition is largely accepted in the Muslim world and is the working definition utilized by the Kingdom. In Islam to term a Muslim as a terrorist is not only a criminal act but an act against Islam.

In the Kingdom extremists and terrorists are often given the moniker of "deviant" or "Kharijite"; they are defined as, "those who corrupt the Islamic faith and pervert Islam to preach

---

[1] King Abdullah bin Abdulaziz. "Royal Embassy of Saudi Arabia: Issue-War on Terrorism.". (*Royal Embassy of Saudi Arabia.* May 13, 2003). http://www.saudiembassy.net/Issues/Terrorism/IssuesTer.asp (accessed 12 January 2009).

[2] Abdullah F. Ansary. "Combating Extremism: A Brief Overview of Saudi Arabia's Approach." (*Middle East Policy* XV, no. 2, Summer 2008), 118.

[3] Brigadier General Ahmed S. Al-Mufarih. *The Role of the Kingdom of Saudi Arabia in Combating Terrorism.* (Strategy Research Project, Carlisle: U.S. Army War College, 2004), 2.

violence."[4] Important to note, the Kingdom does not view the two as synonymous entities. One can be an extremist without being a terrorist and vice versa. This delineation is what has affected the approaches the Kingdom has chosen in order to combat these threats.

The Kingdom is no newcomer to the threats of Islamic extremism and terrorism. It fact, many critics claim the Kingdom gained its authority via a form of Islamic extremism. From its earliest days the Kingdom has combated extremists. In the late 1920's extremism almost leads to the downfall of the Kingdom. Abd al Aziz, first King and founder of the modern Saudi Kingdom, puts down a rebellion by the same Islamic zealots upon whom he depends to aid him in establishing the Kingdom. It is at the Battle of Sabillah in March of 1929 that the future Saudi King defeats the first extremist uprising questioning Al Saud hegemony.[5] This battle puts an end of what is known as the *Ikhwan* Rebellion. [6]

Since that time the Kingdom encounters a few incidents that it attributes to extremist beliefs or terrorist activity. In 1979 the Kingdom confronts an uprising of fundamental Sunnis in Mecca and Shia seeking equal rights in its Eastern Provinces. In the 1990's the Kingdom faced a rash of bombings and attacks focused on the government's support of perceived pro-western policies. It is not until the terrorist attacks in 2003 that the Kingdom's might in combating these elements is accelerated.

---

[4] Ibid., 118 and Yaroslav Trofimov. *The Siege of Mecca: The Forgotten Uprising in Islam's Holiest Shrine and the Birth of Al Qaeda* (New York: Doubleday, 2007), 34. Kharijite is the name of a radical sect of Islam whose believers assassinated the Prophet Mohammed's son-in-law Ali in the year 661; this name has come to mean a deviant from the Islamic religion.

[5] Robert Lacey, *The Kingdom,* (First American Edition 1982, New York: Harcourt Brace Jovanovich, Publishers, 1981), 201-214.

[6] .David Dean Commins, *The Wahhabi Mission and Saudi Arabia* (London; New York: I.B. Tauris, 2006), 80-93. The *Ikhwan* were an extremely fundamental Wahhabi group of Bedouins devoutly loyal to the imposition of harsh Wahhabist beliefs and dedicated to Abd al Aziz. Abd al Aziz would eventually put down a rebellion of the *Ikhwan* in 1928. Abd al Aziz would eventually disband the Ikhwan and remake them as the White Army, called this because of the white robes they were known to wear. Their descendents would go on to become the Saudi Arabian National Guard, the Kings personal army and internal security force.

The government of the Kingdom feels it has done a great deal to counter the effects of Islamic deviants since this time and are adopting many methods in countering extremism and terrorism on the Arabian Peninsula. However, detractors against the Kingdom say this is not the case and that the Saudi government has not done enough to counter these threats. It is for this reason that the purpose of this monograph is to examine the methods and strategies executed by the Kingdom in countering these threats. The question this research will answer is: What policies, practices and strategies employed by the Kingdom of Saudi Arabia are successful in countering the current Islamic extremist/terrorist threat? To answer this question this research will utilize literature written on and in the Kingdom by scholars and authorities in Middle Eastern affairs. This research will develop background on the historical, cultural and religious methods utilized by the Kingdom in dealing with the current extremist/terrorist threats and how these methods have succeeded in thwarting their definition of extremist/terrorist activity.

It is not the intent of this research to disapprove or approve of Kingdom strategies or tactics as much as inform readers about the methods and approaches utilized by the United States' premier Arab/Islamic ally in combating these threats. It is significant that one comprehend the methods developed for countering these threats are unique to the Kingdom. In order to appreciate why the Saudis have chosen these approaches one must first be familiar with Saudi history and their socio-cultural dynamic. This will aid in identifying what the populace believes and how this dynamic affects Kingdom approaches to the problem. Saudis' religion is an integral component of their culture and thus one must gain an appreciation of Islam from the Saudi perspective to truly grasp their rationale and reasoning on the approaches they have decided are best in countering Islamic threats to the Kingdom and the global community.

The Kingdom of Saudi Arabia: An Overview

It is first essential to answer the questions: Who are the people of the Arabian Peninsula? Why is this understanding important to the approaches taken in combating deviants? The simple answer is they are an amalgamation of Arab tribes that roamed the Najd[7] and Arabian Peninsula in the 19th and 20th Century, through a process of political evolution that intertwines Islam and Arab culture, became the Kingdom. The real answer is much more involved and complex involving over 500 years of history. For the sake of brevity the history of Saudi Arabia relevant to this research will only be discussed from circa 19th Century to the present.

It is essential to comprehend the significant influence the Al Saud family has in the Arabian Peninsula, this insight sets the stage for future extremist/terrorist events. Al Saud influence begins in the mid-18th Century but quickly faced challenges and by the later part of the 19th Century the Al Saud find themselves in exile to Kuwait by their rivals, the Al Rashid.[8] At the beginning of the early 20th Century Al Saud dominance in the region reappears with a vengeance. In 1902, the Al Saud capital of Riyadh submits as well as the holy cities of Mecca and Medina in the mid-1920's; ending with the Kingdom of Saudi Arabia, *Al Mamlakah al Arabiyah as Suudiyah*, being unified by King, *Malik*, Abd al Aziz ibn Abd ar Rahman Al Saud on 23 September 1932.[9]

The current Kingdom of Saudi Arabia has a population of 23 million, which includes over 5.3 million non-national residents. Until the mid-1960's the lifestyle was nomadic or semi-nomadic; but, with rapid economic prosperity came rapid urban growth, today about 95 percent of the population is settled.[10] This growth and modernization, as well as, the influx of non-nationals

---

[7] William Smyth, Eleanor Abdella Doumato, Fareed Mohamedi, Eric Hooglund, and Jean R. Tartter. *Saudi Arabia: A Country Study.* Fifth Edition. Ed. Helen Chapin Metz. (Washington, D.C.: Library of Congress, 1993), 18. The Najd or Nejd is the desert region in the center of the Arabian Peninsula or also known as Central Arabia; it is also the ancestral home of the Al-Saud. The rest of the peninsula is made up of the Hijaz, Rub Al Khali (Empty Quarter), Yemen, Asir, Hadhramaut and the Trucial Coast. See map Appendix B, Fig. 2.

[8] Lacey, 24. The Al Rashid was an influential Najd tribe that opposed Al Saud hegemony and wrested control from them in the latter part of the 19th Century.

[9] Prior to this unification Abd al Aziz was known by the title of "King of the Hejaz and Sultan of the Najd and its Dependencies". David M. Burke, "Saudi Security: Challenges for the Post-Saddam Era" (master's thesis, Naval Postgraduate School, 2004), 7.

[10] Countrywatch. "Saudi Arabia-2008 Country Review." *countrywatch.com.* (2008), under "Saudi Arabia", http://www.countrywatch.com/saudi arabia (accessed October 2, 2008), 113.

contributes to the Kingdoms internal security concerns and paved the way for 'deviant' Islamic movements in the Kingdom. The significance in comprehending how the Kingdom of Saudi Arabia originated is critical to gain full appreciation of how the Kingdom deals with this form of behavior from past to present. This understanding will aid in answering the question: How does the Kingdom view the current extremist/terrorist threat? Though it may seem odd to many westerners, the Saudis have a deeper understanding of the threat they face and through this understanding is why they have taken certain approaches when dealing with the current extremist/terrorist dilemma.

The Ascendancy of the Al Saud and the Evolution of the Contemporary Saudi State

Prior to the establishment of the monarchy by King Abd al Aziz in 1932, there are pivotal events that substantiate the Al Saud family as the dominant family of all the Arab tribes on the peninsula. For over 200 years the Al Saud family continues to perform a key role in the Arabian Peninsula. The history of this ascendancy to power can best be explained within the description of three separate dynastic periods. The significance of the origins of the Saudi State is that through their origins come the formation of contemporary Kingdom policy and socio-cultural reaction to dealing with the current domestic threats posed by extremists and terrorists.

The First Dynasty, 1745-1818, of the Al Saud begins with Muhammad ibn Saud ibn Mugrin[11] in his conquest of the Arabian Peninsula in the late 18th Century. Muhammad ibn Saud was aided in his conquest by Muhammad ibn Abd al Wahhab[12]; the relationship between Muhammad ibn Saud and Muhammad ibn Abd al Wahhab set the stage for the unification of the

---

[11] Smyth and Metz, 13-16. The title Saudi is derived from its namesake Saud ibn Muhammad ibn Muqrin, the father of Muhammad ibn Saud, the progenitor of the Al Saud Royal family. In contradiction to Arab culture, the name has become synonymous with the citizens of the Kingdom of Saudi Arabia.

[12] Ibid., 14. It is from him that the term *Wahhabi* is derived. This name is not what the Saudis call their sect of Islam; though they are proponents to the tenets set by Muhammad ibn Abd al Wahhab, 1703-97, they, as he did, refer to themselves as *Muwahhidun* or Unitarians. It is the detractors of this sect that refer to them as Wahabbis.

tribes on the Arabian Peninsula and the establishment of the religious and political might of Islam that will eventually propel the Al Saud to be the preeminent Muslim monarchy the contemporary world has seen.[13]

Muhammad ibn Abd al Wahhab, 1703-97, is a Muslim scholar and founder of the *Muwahhidun* (Unitarian) movement or more commonly known as Wahabbis. He studied Hanbali Islamic Law[14] and went on to establish a sect of Islam where strict adherence to the principles of *Sharia*, Islamic Law, is a must. He directed his attack against Shia Muslims due to their belief in what he referred to as popular Islam or *Shirk*, polytheism[15]. He believed himself to be the reformer of Islam and sought to solidify his position by seeking a strong political figure upon which he could depend to spread his message. Muhammad ibn Abd al Wahhab is credited with being the first Muslim scholar and Imam to attach political importance to his view of Islam.[16] He is forced out of Eastern Arabia by dominant Shia authorities due to his anti-Shia rhetoric and escapes to Ad Diriyah, the Riyadh area of the Najd. In 1744, after years of seeking a political supporter, he finds one in Muhammad ibn Saud. He and Al Saud swear an oath to establish a state ruled according to Islamic principles.[17] What Wahhab did was define a clear religious mission to which the Al Saud can then base their political authority.

---

[13] Commins, 7-39. In order to truly grasp Al Saud hegemony, one has to understand the special relationship built between the Al Wahhab(also known as Al Shaykh) and Al Saud families. You cannot have one without the other.

[14] Doumato and Metz, 79-80. There are four Sunni legal schools of Islam: The Hanafi, Maliki, Muhammad in Idris ash Shafii and Hanbali. Hanbali is considered one of the strictest forms of Muslim legal schooling. It is considered the hardest in terms of social and personal rules. Founded by Imam Ahmad ibn Hanbal (circa 9th Century) imprisoned over the controversy regarding whether the Quran was "uncreated" or subject to the interpretations of man. Hanbali believers believe that the Quran is the unequivocal word of Allah and man has no right to stray from its word. However an important principle is that it allows for things to be assumed pure or allowable unless first proved otherwise.

[15] Smyth and Metz, 12. Popular Islam is also known as non-universal Islam and *Shirk* mainly refers to the Shia practices of visiting shrines and the reverence or worship given to Imams after their death, also the celebration of the Prophets birthday; in Christianity this would amount to saint worship.

[16] Commins, 17.

[17] Smyth and Metz, 15.

With this new found authority, Muhammad ibn Saud begins to lead armies into the

Arabian Peninsula in order to subdue other popular and Shia practices. He does so until his death

in 1765 when his son Abd al Aziz ibn Muhammad continues the advance. With the death of

Muhammad al Wahhab in 1792 the Al Saud not only claim the leadership title of *Shaykh,* leader,

but also the religious title of *Imam.* This is significant in that not only does this recognize the Al

Saud as political leaders but also as religious authorities; first time in Arab history that this is

accomplished.[18] In 1801, the Al Saud-Al Wahhab armies advance into Iraq and destroy Karbala,

the Shia holy site in Iraq, and the tomb of Hussayn, grandson of the Prophet. Their destruction of

Karbala is to imitate the Prophet Muhammad's destruction of pagan idols when he reentered

Mecca in 630.[19] By 1803, they conquer the holy cities of Mecca and Medina, where they destroy

shrines and even plunder the tomb of the Prophet Muhammad.

This conquest continues into the 19th Century with the son of Abd al Aziz, Saud, taking

the reins from his father in 1814; in that same year Saud dies and his son Abd Allah becomes

Imam. Abd Allah faces the largest threat to the Al Saud in the form of an invading Egyptian

Army determined to re-establish control over the peninsula for the Ottoman Sultan. This is due to

the Al Saud /Wahhabi capture of the two holy cities of Mecca and Medina in 1803. This reaction

of the Ottoman Sultan, also known as the Caliph or leader of all Muslims, is a devastating insult

to the Caliph. That these two cities are under the control of this religious group is considered by

most Muslims of the time to be heretical.[20]

By 1811 Sultan Mahmud II tires of Al Saud insolence and decides to take decisive action.

This same year he sends instructions to the viceroy of Egypt, Muhammad Ali, to invade the

Arabian Peninsula and retake the Hijaz or western region of the Arabian Peninsula. By the end of

1815 the Egyptian Army reclaims the two holy cities for the Caliph and, by1818, the Egyptians

---

[18] Ibid., 17.

[19] Ibid., 15. The significance of this act is it provides the roots for the animus that exists between Shia and Sunnis in the region and especially in the Kingdom.

[20] Burke, 8.

fight through to the Najd and defeat the Al Saud at their capital in Ad Diriyah. Abd Allah is sent to Istanbul and executed. This defeat ends the First Saud Dynasty.

The Second Saud Dynasty, 1824-1891, begins with the rise of Turki ibn Abd Allah, grandson of Muhammad Ibn Saud, and his defiance of Ottoman and Egyptian rule. In 1819 the Egyptians remove a majority of their forces from the Najd. With Egyptian hold over the Najd weakening, in 1824, Turki begins to reestablish Al Saud influence in the region and conquest of the Najd and the Eastern Provinces. In 1834 he is assassinated and his son Faisal is proclaimed *Imam*. In 1835, Muhammad Ali, turns on the Ottomans and attempts to establish Egyptian hegemony of the region. Faisal refuses to join forces with him and in 1838 is removed from power and his cousin Khalid is placed in charge. Faisal escapes from prison in 1843 and reclaims his position as Saudi *Imam*.[21] Upon Faisal's death in 1865 his son Abd Allah becomes ruler. His reign is marked by infighting within the family and the forming and reforming of alliances within the tribes, the Al Saud's authority on the peninsula becomes unstable and is left ripe for regime change. Abd Allah asks for Ottoman intervention to oust his brother Saud who wrested control from Abd Allah in 1870.[22] The Ottomans are pleased to come to his aid and help reestablish Abd Allah as the rightful leader. The civil war within the Al Saud pave the way for the Al Rashid rise to power and by 1891 they seize control of Riyadh and emplace a puppet Al Saud faction to rule, Abd ar Rahman father of the future King Abd al Aziz. When Abd ar Rahman attempts to enforce true authority, the Al Saud family is exiled to Kuwait.[23]

The Third Saud Dynasty begins, in 1891 and exists to the present day. This dynastic period manifests in Kuwait with Abd al Aziz ibn Abd ar Rahman, the founder of the modern Saudi state, preparing to restore Al Saud hegemony on the peninsula. Due to his charisma and ability to influence the Bedouin tribes he is able to create an army that returns the Al Saud as the

---

[21] Ibid., 10.

[22] Ibid., 11

[23] For a full explanation of events that transpire in this period see Smyth and Metz, 16-20.

prominent tribe on the Arabian Peninsula. In 1902, his armies recapture the city of Riyadh with help from the *Ikhwan*, brotherhood, and defeat elements of the Al Rashid. He continues his conquest with aid from the Ottoman Empire and the British. By the late 1920's he secures his rule over most of the Arabian Peninsula. In 1927 the first test on Abd al Aziz's authority results in what becomes known as the *Ikhwan* rebellion.

The *Ikhwan* are true Wahhabi zealots, many argue the first extremists/terrorists organization in the contemporary Saudi state- the Arabian Peninsula at this time is not the unified Kingdom. They are unhappy with Abd al Aziz's compromise with the British Empire[24] and begin a bloody campaign of retribution on non-Wahhabi Muslims in the area. Abd al Aziz routes the *Ikhwan* in March 1929 at the Battle of Sabillah by dealing a demoralizing blow to the *Ikhwan* when one of their legendary tribal leaders, Faisal al Duwaish, is quickly wounded.[25] This incident and the mere fact that the Al Saud is better equipped quickly ends the battle and effectively quells the uprising. Duwaish and Bijad are imprisoned and quickly die thereafter. The rest of the *Ikhwan* encampments, known as *hijras*[26], are gutted and many of the families are consumed by infighting. Abd al Aziz reestablishes order in the Najd and establishes the Kingdom of Saudi Arabia in 1932. The *Ikhwan* rebellion is the birth of Kingdom extremists threats that will come back to haunt the Al Saud.

---

[24] Trofimov, 17-18. Abd al Aziz understands that he cannot go to war with the British and makes treaties with them which allow for the unmolested movement of non-Wahhabi Muslims in the Trans Jordan area, Iraq, Kuwait and the Arabian Peninsula. The *Ikhwan* see this as an affront to their religious beliefs and break these treaties by attacking British subjects. They conduct cross border raids into Trans Jordan, Iraq and Kuwait; killing many non-Wahhabis under British protection and thus incurring the wrath of the British Empire. In order to appease the British, Abd al Aziz, begins to allow British Royal Air Force bombing sorties against *Ikhwan* camps and conducts a campaign to bring the *Ikhwan* back under his authority.

[25] Ibid. Faisal al Duwaish and Sultan al Bijad are the two preeminent tribal leader of the Uteybi Tribe. This tribe provides many of the *Ikhwan* soldiers. Even today the Uteybi are a major tribe with immense influence in the Saudi Arabian National Guard.

[26] Ibid., 16-18. *Hijra* literally means migration but became synonymous with the settlements of *Ikhwan*. It will be a a hijra in northern Riyadh that one of the veterans of the Battle of Sabillah, Mohammed bin Seif al Uteybi, who fought side by side with Bijad and remembered his final words: "Never give up" will become father to a son by the name of Juhayman.

King Abd al Aziz is nothing like his predecessors. He understands the intricacies of the environment in which he lives and capitalizes on them. He realizes a major threat to Al Saud hegemony is familial infighting. Infighting he views as a detriment to the Al Saud tribe and employs different strategies to ensure stability. One of his strategies is that of intermarriage amongst the family branches. He also posts senior members from other family branches to key governmental positions; as well as, set the precedent for the Kingdom's alliances with foreign powers in which to enhance its security. Abd al Aziz begins to cultivate relations with the British and ultimately the United States. Both these relationships remain today.

After his death in 1958 he is succeeded by his son Saud and every king thereafter is a direct son of Abd al Aziz.[27] Saud rules till1964 and is succeeded by his brother Faisal in 1964. The rule of Saud is tumultuous, at best, due to his mismanagement of the government and allowing the Kingdom to become a sideshow to his own personal life. He ignores much of his societal demands and treats his rule of the Kingdom as more of a nuisance than a duty. He is replaced by his brother Faisal, who is seen as the best candidate to progress the Kingdom into the 20th Century.

Faisal's ascension to the throne is gained by a *fatwa*, religious ruling, from the *Ulema*. This is an important event, in that, it marks the first time in Kingdom history that the religious elite overrules a son of Abd al Aziz and in essence replaces the rightful heir with the heir apparent.[28] Faisal becomes one of the most prosperous rulers for the Kingdom. It is during his reign that the Kingdom is to reemerge as the dominant oil broker in the Middle East as well as enter into a modernization and reform program; the effects of which are still being seen to present day. Faisal is assassinated in 1975 by a nephew and his replacement is his brother Khalid who comes to power due to the current crown prince, Muhammed bin Abd al Aziz, abdicating the throne to him.

---

[27] For a genealogy of succession to the present day see Appendix A.

[28] Lacey, 353-354.

Khalid is not much interested in politics and effectively relinquishes rule to Crown Prince

Fahd.[29] During his reign the Kingdom gains unprecedented economic prosperity. He also faces

the reemergence of Islamic traditionalism/extremism, epitomized by the 1979 uprising at the

Grand Mosque in Mecca and the Shia uprising in the Eastern Province.

On Tuesday, 20 November 1979, Sunni Wahhabi zealots believing the return of the

Mahdi[30], redeemer, assault and occupy the Grand Mosque in Mecca. The leader of this uprising is

a former Saudi Arabian National Guard, SANG, Corporal by the name of Juhayman.[31] Juhayman

and his followers detest Westernization and the way they believe Saudi society is heading. They

derive their inspiration from old *Ikhwan* ideals and the recent Iranian revolution by Ayatollah

Khomeini[32] Juhayman's intent is to bring the downfall of the house of Saud. He sees the Al Saud

as pawns of the West and deviators from the teachings of Muhammad ibn Abd al Wahhab. As a

---

[29] Ibid., 68 and 174. Fahd was the eldest of the "Sudairi Seven", a moniker referring to seven sons of Abd al Aziz by Hussah bint Ahmad Al Sudairi. Abd al Aziz's mother was also a Sudairi. The seven brothers, the largest contingent of sons of Abd al Aziz, aided each other's political careers and were acknowledged as being the most powerful group within the Al Saud family. Among his full brothers, Prince Sultan bin Abd al Aziz has been the Minister of Defense and Aviation since 1962 and Second Deputy Prime Minister since 1982; he is currently also the Crown Prince. Prince Nayif bin Abd al Aziz, who succeeded Fahd as Interior Minister in 1975, Prince Salman bin Abd al Aziz, the Governor of Riyadh, and Deputy Interior Minister Prince Ahmed are also considered potential future kings.

[30] Trofimov, 45-52. The legend of the *Mahdi* or redeemer is not found in the *Quran* but has been foretold by some Muslim scholars as the coming of a redeemer sent by God to right the world and make it a just Muslim society. He will bring peace and justice. He will be known, in that, he will look like the Prophet Mohammad, have a fair complexion and a large birthmark on his cheek, he will be tall and come from the Quraysh tribe, tribe of the Prophet. He is to receive the *baya* on the holiest of ground, the Kabaa right after the Hajj at the turn of a new Muslim century. In 1978 the Muslim calendar was turning from 1398 to 1399.

[31] Ibid., 18. His father was a follower of Sheykh Bijad during the *Ikhwan* Rebellion. Juhayman broke with the Saudi *Ulema* after a 1977 meeting where the senior clerics were deciding what was religiously best for the Kingdom. Their outcome was that the Al Saud was better than the rest and this enraged Juhayman. He openly crosses into sedition and proclaims that to be a true ruler of Muslims one had to be a Muslim, be a member of the Al Quraysh [Prophet Mohammad's tribe], and be a man who applies religion. He points out that the monarchy is only the first of the three. He also makes claim that a Muslim scholar in the Kingdom has only three options: agree with Al Saud, remain quiet, or oppose the regime. He chooses the latter, Ibid., 33-34.

[32] Lacey, 481-482. Juhayman and his followers were by no means adherents of the Ayatollah but they gained inspiration for their cause through the Ayatollah's actions that showed how a man preaching the word of God could bring down a mighty ruler such as the Shah.

former student of Sheykh Abd al Aziz bin Baz[33], Chairman of Saudi Arabia's Department of

Scientific Research and Guidance, Juhayman sees himself as a reformer to bring the Kingdom

back to its conservative Wahhabi values and the guardian of the *Mahdi*, whom he identifies as

Muhammad ibn Abd Allah al Qahtani, a former university student he claims to see in a dream

which revealed him as the *Mahdi*. To his dismay, almost none of the thousands of Muslims he

confines in the Grand Mosque want anything to do with the proclaimed *Mahdi*. The Kingdom

does not rise in response to his calls for reform and with that his revolt is in ruins. After ten days

of fighting he and those of his followers still alive are arrested. Sixty three prisoners are executed;

Juhayman is the first.[34]

The outcome of this uprising effects are felt in the Kingdom today. It is because of this

uprising the Kingdom reverses their modernizing ways. King Khaled, in return for *Ulema*

support, compromises with Bin Baz and other senior clerics and begins the imposition of strict

adherence to Wahhabi fundamental beliefs. Women bear a good brunt of this compromise and

their liberties are restricted. The Committee to Promote Virtue and Prevent Vice, *Mutawaa*, is

given broader leeway when dealing with Westerners and instilling Wahabbi orthodoxy. Alcohol

is another target, which in itself is against the practices of Muslims, had been overlooked in years

past now became *haram*, forbidden. The Saudi government's stance is to embrace Wahhabi

orthodoxy to the extent that besides the belief in a *Mahdi* is exactly what Juhayman wanted.[35] In

2004, Prince Khalid al Faisal, governor of Asir states, "I believe we have made a mistake in this

Kingdom…We have eliminated the individuals who committed the Juyhaman crime, but we have

---

[33] Trofimov, ix. This is a ministerial level clerical body in charge of interpreting Islamic law. Bin Baz, as he is often referred, started his early protests in the 1940's. He expressed the same objections to Western influences as did Al Qaeda is voicing today. Jailed by King Abd al Aziz for opposing royal policy, he was later released and through a lengthy career he would always temper his criticisims of modernazation by backing the Al Saud regime in times of adversity.

[34] Ibid., 239.

[35] Ibid., 243

overlooked the ideology that was behind the crime. We let it spread in the country, ignoring it as it if it did not exist."[36]

Consequently, in December of 1979 the Shia in the Eastern Province riot against inequality. Though not related to Juhayman's siege of the Grand Mosque they do share similar inspiration due to the Ayatollah's Iranian revolution. The Saudi Shia are not trying to seek a separate state but seek equality within the Kingdom.[37] Many Saudi Shia return from Karbela with propaganda to rise against the tyranny oppressing them; this all comes to a head during the first month of the Islamic new year, *Muharram*. The Saudi Shia utilize this fervor to march in processions commemorating the death of the Prophet's grandson Hussayn. This procession is a Shia tradition which has been banned by the Al Saud in order not to provoke Wahhabi beliefs. The Shia underestimate the Kingdom's response and SANG responds vehemently and puts down the riots. Many Shia are killed and jailed. By the end of December 1979 the Eastern Province is quieted and this the Saudi government begins rebuilding the Kingdom's security apparatus to insure against these types of incidents in the future.[38] King Khalid dies in 1982 and is succeeded by his brother Fahd.

Fahd rules the Kingdom till his death in 2005. During his reign he is held responsible by Osama bin Laden and Al Qaeda for being the catalyst that unites Muslim extremist and terrorist against the Al Saud royal family and the west. King Fahd becomes a staunch supporter of the U.S. led coalition in 1991 to oust the Iraqi Army out of Kuwait during Operation Desert Storm. He suffers a stroke in 1995 and effective rule of the Kingdom resides with then sitting Crown Prince Abd Allah who becomes King upon Fahd's death.

---

[36] Ibid.

[37] Lacey, 489. This inequity goes back centuries. The Eastern Province at this time is almost like a fiefdom run by Abd Allah bin Jaluwi and his sons. The Eastern Province was traditionally kept docile by the Jaluwis and remained underdeveloped.

[38] Ibid., 489-490.

The current ruler of the Kingdom is His Royal Highness (HRH) and Custodian of the two Holy Mosques, King Abd Allah bin Abd al Aziz. He continues to lead the Kingdom into the new millennium and is a staunch ally of the U.S. led Global War on Terror (GWOT). His reforms and progressive attitude have become at odds with certain members of the ruling elite. He is said to be a believer in the concept of *Taqarub*, accomadation or living in harmony with non-Muslims, versus the much more traditional Wahabbi belief of *Tawhid*, uncompromising monotheism, which its advocates utilize *takfir*, labeling of fellow Muslims as apostates, if they choose to deviate from the approved Wahhabi message of strict adherence to the Islamic version of God.[39] To date he is an advocate for reform and Saudization, or the restoration of Saudi citizens to the professional workforce within the Kingdom. The issue of Saudization is a major concern in reinvigorating support for Al Saud rule and is also the main argument of Saudis who are at odds with the current government. This issue is a priority for King Abd Allah and influences the strategies the Kingdom utilizes to combat deviant threats.

A major concern for the Al Saud is many conservative and progressive Saudis see the Al Saud family as being an outdated and corrupt regime.[40] There are many who want to see the rule of the Al Saud abolished and see a conservative Islamic state emplaced in its absence, this concern is why the monarchy maintains formidable internal security measures. The difficulty with this notion owes to the lack of consensus on what a replacement government would be or who would best be able to control the Arabian Peninsula. Since 1932, the Kingdom has been an absolute monarchy ruled by the male members of the Al Saud family or more precisely the hereditary sons of Abd al Aziz. The sons of the first king, Abd al Aziz ibn Abd ar Rahman, are currently the sole heirs to the throne.[41] The king's decree is law. He is both head of state and head

---

[39] Sherifa Zuhur. *Saudi Arabia: Islamic Threat, Political Reform and the Global War on Terror* (SSI Monograph, Carlisle: Strategic Studies Institute, U.S. Army War College, 2005), 16-17.

[40] Ibid., 32-38.

[41] Burke, 39-40. This form of succession is becoming an issue within the royal family as the sons of Abd al Aziz become smaller in number. King Fahd established the *Bayah* Council in the 1990's to look

of government. He maintains a Council of Ministers, created by King Abd al Aziz in 1953 prior to his death, which has the authority to issue ministerial decrees but only with the approval of the sitting monarch. The main focus for the government is on internal issues not foreign policy. Because of the Kingdom's small population and size and the effectiveness of its security forces and military, it approaches many of its external issues through the cultural and religious fundamentals of patience, persistence and negotiation; usually behind closed doors.[42]

The organization of the Council of Ministers consists of the king, the crown prince, three royal advisers, five ministers of state and 20 other ministries. The crown prince also holds the title of first deputy prime minister with the next prince in the line of succession as the second deputy prime minister.[43] Currently the crown prince and first prime minister is HRH Crown Prince Sultan ibn Abd al Aziz who is also the minister of the Ministry of Defense and Aviation, Saudi version of the U.S. Department of Defense. The second deputy prime minister is currently HRH Prince Nayif ibn Abd al Aziz, the minister of the Ministry of the Interior; responsible for the internal security of the Kingdom. Some argue he is the most powerful prince in the Kingdom and more influential than the crown prince.

Together with the monarchy and the Council of Ministers are the *Ulema* or religious council. This group once exercised enormous influence on matters concerning the state but has been in decline over the past few decades. Much of this decline is due in response to their ultra conservative slant after the 1979 uprising that some argue paved the way for Al Qaeda. The *Ulema* are religious scholars who trace their descent to Al Wahhab or the supporters of his teachings. This group decides which laws are in compliance with *Sharia* Law. The Kingdom takes great pride in being an Islamic state.

---

into new rules of succession that would allow male members of the royal family to be chosen as heir after the rule of the next king. On 1 March 1992 he enacted the Law of Government which describes the system of government and the rules for succession.

[42] John Peterson. *Saudi Arabia and the Illlusion of Security* (London: Oxford University Press for the International Institute for Strategic Studies, 2002), 30.

[43] Countrywatch. 53-58.

Of particular note in relation to the authority of the monarchy are the tribes and how their association with the Al Saud family aid in Al Saud hegemony of the Arabian tribes on the peninsula. The tribes of Saudi Arabia acknowledge the political authority of the monarchy as being above their own tribal groups.[44] Though, loyalty to the state is a more modern notion that is catching on with younger Saudi generations; as far as the tribes are concerned, their loyalties are to the Al Saud family not necessarily the state. The loyalty the tribes have given the Al Saud is based on the concept of the Islamic nation and the security the monarchy provides in assuring its existence.

The Saud family is often placed under scrutiny because the Kingdom is under its absolute rule. This fact leads to the contentious issue of disenfranchisement. Many of the youth believe there is a dual law system that exists within the Kingdom. This dissent is detrimental to Al Saud hegemony remaining in place. It is also one of the major concerns for security within the Kingdom and one of the main places extremists and terrorists find recruits.

According to Sherifa Zuhur, author of *Saudi Arabia: Islamic Threat, Political Reform, and the Global War on Terror*, "young people, speaking anonymously, saying that there are two laws in the country; one for the ruled and one for the rulers."[45] This is indicative of the growing dissent of the younger generation. Familial patronage, *wasta*, is a fundamental aspect to Arab culture and this cultural norm is what is being affected by the size of the Al Saud family.[46] In a system where the patronage system is a prevailing feature of life, any threat to this system is a fundamental threat to the Kingdom. Within the *wasta* system lie the informal, pragmatic and trusted methods of lobbying, mediating and distributing political goods.[47] Much of the technical workforce in the Kingdom is outsourced to foreigners, in recent years Saudi disenfranchisement

---

[44] Doumato and Metz, 69-70. The sheykhs of the tribes continue to support the Al Saud as long as the Al Saud appease the tribes concerns.

[45] Zuhur, 10.

[46] Ibid.

[47] Ibid.

has led to internal security concerns in countering extremist rhetoric calling for dissolution of the royal family and a reversion to a totalitarian Islamic state.

The inequity of financial resources continues to be a grave source of discord within the Kingdom with many extremist and moderate reformers. It is due to this concern; King Abd Allah has taken measures to redistribute wealth amongst the royal family as well reinvigorate the Saudi workforce. He has begun internal programs to re-Saudize the Kingdom's industry through offering professional skills education and academic education opportunities to offer Saudi citizens a way to progress into the modern world.[48] King Abd Allah understands that in order to counter deviant behavior he must appease his citizenry. He accomplishes this by remaining true to the Arab custom of allegiance or *bayah*. It is the responsibility of the Al Saud to provide for the prosperity and security of the tribes. Above all King Abd Allah understands that allegiances within the Arab tribes are earned not given.

What it means to be a Saudi Arabian

It is not an Arab norm to concede ones tribe to the rule of a single family or person.[49] Therefore, it is of the utmost importance that one comprehends the significance that this is what Abd al Aziz accomplished. Arabs are extremely proud people and it took a man of incredible charisma and influences to bring them together and form the Kingdom. His ancestors never accomplished what he did. This is due to their lack of strategic vision in unifying the Arab people and strengthening their position in the region by becoming an established Arab nation. Abd al Aziz understood the nuisances of what it would take to unify the tribes as a state and utilized this understanding to solidify his position as not only King of the Najd but most of the Arabian Peninsula as the king of unified Arab state under rule of the Al Saud. It is important to understand

[48] Anthony H. Cordesman and Nawaf Obaid. *Saudi Counter Terrorism Efforts: The Changing Paramilitary and Domestic Security Apparatus* (Washington, D.C.: Center for Strategic and International Studies, 2005), 20. As of February 2005 the Saudization program has just begun to meet internal stability and security means. Saudis filled only 13% of the 45% recommended.

[49] Doumato and Metz, 69-71.

who the Arabs are as a people so that we can better understand why it is they believe what they do and approach deviants the way they have.

The people of Saudi Arabia are commonly referred to as Saudis; this is a misnomer. To truly be a Saudi refers to being a descendant of the Al Saud family. With the establishment of the Kingdom and the evolution of Saudi Arabia as a nation state; the fact the people of the Kingdom adopts the familial name of their monarch to refer to themselves as a whole is proper and in contradiction to Arab custom.[50] Arabs are very proud people and familial and tribal ties mean everything. Ethnically and culturally the people of Saudi Arabia are Arabs or Bedouins, the nomadic tribes that roamed the Arabian Peninsula, much akin to Native Americans.[51]

The term Arab, refers to the genealogical lineage of the tribes that inhabited the Arabian Peninsula and Syria in pre-Islamic times, as well as, to those who speak the Arabic language. It is important to understand that to be considered Arab is not merely an ethnic, religious, or cultural identity but most importantly a lingual identity.[52] The majority of native Saudi people trace their heritage to the early Arab/Bedouin tribes; though the current Kingdom of Saudi Arabia is much more diverse in its demographic.

The most important social institution in the Kingdom is the family or tribe. Familial and tribal ties mean everything. Alignments are formed through inter and intra marriage with families that share common lifestyles and interests. This is important to note, in that, loyalties to family and members of one's tribe usually supersede that of the state. Tribes are patriarchal in construct with each tribe answering to a *shaykh*. The *shaykh* in turn governs by consensus and gains influence through his ability to mediate; essentially he is arbitrator and is usually effective as long as he conforms to the tribe's expectations.

---

[50] Ibid., 70.

[51] Raphael Patai, *The Arab Mind*, Revised 1983 edition (New York: Hatherleigh Press, 2002), 78. Today only about 10 percent of the Arab world can claim Bedouin status.

[52] For a detailed explanation of what is an Arab see Ibid., 9-15.

Arab culture is prominent in the norms and mores of the Kingdoms citizenry. Though Islam is infused with the culture to make the two indistinguishable there are prevailing Arab ethics that Saudis hold dear that pre-date Islam. Raphael Patai summarizes these ethics in his book, *The Arab Mind*. He argues there are three syndromes which best describe Arab virtue: the courage-bravery syndrome; the hospitality-generosity syndrome; the honor-dignity syndrome.[53] The values expressed in each of these syndromes are crucial in understanding how peninsular Arabs view themselves. Saudis, as do other Arabs, hold the virtues of bravery and manliness, hospitality and generosity, and the honor syndrome in the highest of regard. Important to note is that these ethics of virtue are not part of the ethical system of the *Quran*, thus distinguishing Arab culture from Islamic culture. In fact, Arab culture surpasses Quranic culture in the institution of these virtues. The only virtue which is equitably shared by both is sexual modesty of women or *fitna,* sexual temptation, which is usually attributed to women.[54] When it is all boiled down, the main moral aim of the Arab is the preservation of self-respect. This above all else is paramount: the importance of being respected by others.[55]

Today, the people of Saudi Arabia are an amalgamation of peoples from diverse ethnicities and races. Saudi Arabia has residents from Africa, Asia, and Western nations. The binding factor that makes all Saudi citizens equal is that they speak Arabic, accept the Al Saud as their protectors and believe in the religion of Islam. For years, there has been growing tensions in the Kingdom based on this dynamic and external influence. Many young Saudis are seeking a modern state while there are opponents who seek to revert back to an earlier age where *sharia* law is the only law that no government or monarchy can dispute. This latter attitude is best observed from the teachings and books written by Sheykh Abd al Aziz bin Baz, once Chairman of Saudi Arabia's Department of Scientific Research and Guidance. Sheykh bin Baz's teachings

---

[53] Ibid., 103-104.

[54] Doumato and Metz, 67. This objectification of women is not uncommon to the Arabs or the Middle East; though it is seen as being subjugating too many Western societies.

[55] For more information on this subject see Patai, 105-107.

and those of other traditional Wahhabi scholars give rise to the reformist movement or Neo-Ikhwan within the Kingdom.[56] These diverging opinions create much of the internal strife within the Kingdom's religious community.

Islam and the Kingdom

The most important guideline for social life within the Kingdom is religion. Islam influences all aspects of Saudi and Muslim culture and it is the cornerstone of Saudi identity. As stated, the special relationship between the Al Saud and Al Wahhab families is the catalyst responsible for the formation of the Kingdom. The allegiance between these two families led to the first institution of Islam, not only as, a unifying state religion but as a political power. The Kingdom not only holds the distinction of being the birthplace of Islam but is also seen as the guardian of two of its holiest sites, Mecca and Medina. This exclusive association affects Kingdom policies and practices in that the Kingdom only recognizes, "the one true religion"; Islam. To have an appreciation for what drives fundamental Islamic beliefs is to have insight into the heart of the Kingdom's decision making process.

There are two preeminent divisions of Islam, Sunni and Shia. Both sects are practiced within the Kingdom with the majority of Muslims in the Kingdom being Sunni or more precisely Sunni Wahabbi. The fundamental split between Sunni and Shia is in the belief of separation with regards to Imam Ali, son-in-law of the Prophet. In essence, the Sunnis believe there are no hereditary heirs to the Prophet Muhammad; whereas, the Shia believe that all Imams must trace their heritage to Imam Ali through his son Husayn.[57]

Islam is established by the Prophet Muhammad in the early 7th Century in the town of Mecca. It is there that he receives the *shahada*, testimony, which explicitly states the central

---

[56] Trofimov, 27-30.

[57] For a full explanation of the two sects see Doumato and Metz, 74-77.

belief of Islam, "There is no god but God and Muhammad is his Prophet". Islam means submission to God and one who submits is a Muslim.

In 613 A.D. Muhammad receives a series of revelations by God through the angel Gabriel that stress monotheism and denounce polytheism.[58] His followers compile his teachings, which they believe come directly from Allah, into the *Quran*, literally translated as recitation, the holy book of Islam. Other teachings and sayings of the Prophet are published in the *hadith*, which serve as the basis of Islamic law. The precedent of his personal deeds and utterances are published as the *sunna*. These three manuscripts serve as the comprehensive guide to the spiritual, ethical and social life of orthodox Sunni Muslims. All Sunni Muslims believe in the Five Pillars of Faith, *Arkan al Islam*: The pronouncement of oneness with god/*Shahada*, Prayer /*Salat*, Fasting/*Sawm*, Almsgiving/*Zakat* and the Pilgrimage/*Hajj*.[59] These are seen as the five most important obligations of a Sunni Muslim. The Shia deviate in that not only do they incorporate the Five Pillars, which they call the 'principles of religion', but add an additional three.[60]

Earlier the origin of what has become known as Wahabbism is detailed. To reiterate, the term Wahabbi is a derogatory term originally used by the enemies of the *Muwahhidun*. Today it has become commonplace and is even used by some of the movements own scholars. To understand Wahabbism is to understand the what and the why of fundamental Saudi Islamic belief. The *Muwahhidun*/Wahabbist movement is a puritanical form of Sunni Islam founded by Muhammad ibn Abd al Wahhab. The adherents of this sect believe themselves to be the only true Muslims. The central theme to the *Muwahhidun* movement is the *tawhid*, essential oneness with

---

[58] 622 A.D. is recognized as the *hijrah* or emigration and it is the chronological date which muslims trace their calendar. This is done by the lunar calendar of 354 days. see Marmaduke William Pickthall, trans., *The Koran*. Ninth Printing (New York: Alfred A. Knopf, 1992), xiii.

[59] Patai, 162.

[60] Important.ca. *Five Pillars of Islam*. 2005. http://www.important.ca/five_pillars_of_islam.html (accessed December 13, 2008). The first is *jihad*, which is also important to the Sunni, but not considered a pillar. The second is *Amr-Bil-Ma'ruf*, the "Enjoining to Do Good", which calls for every Muslim to live a virtuous life and to encourage others to do the same. The third is *Nahi-Anil-Munkar*, the "Exhortation to Desist from Evil", which tells Muslims to refrain from vice and from evil actions and to encourage others to do the same.

God or uncompromising monotheism. Its discipiles refer to it as *ad dawa lil tawhid*, the call to unity, and those who follow the call are known *asahl at tawhid* , the people of unity, or *muwahhidun* .[61]

The emphasis on *tawhid* is in opposition to *shirk*, further defined as any act associating any person, object or thing with powers that are only those of God. The condemnation of acts such as sectarian offerings, praying at graves or saints' tombs, ritual prayer to a third party to intercede with God is considered *haram*, forbidden. Particularly heinous are certain religious festivals, such as celebrating the Prophets Birthday, Shia mourning ceremonies, and Sufi mysticism. The condemnation of *shirk* is the movements main focus as is the literal interpretation of the *Quran* and *sunna*. This puritanical view of Islam is what sets the Sunni Wahabbist aside from moderate and reform Muslims.[62]

In the Kingdom, Wahhabism is synonymous with *Salafiyya or Salafi*, follow or precede, movement; a reference to the followers of the Prophet Muhammad. Many Muslims consider Wahhabism to be Saudi Arabia's form of *Salafiyya*.[63] Unlike Wahabbism the modern *Salafi* movement grew from reform oriented Muslims in the late 19th early 20th Century. This movement has grown more conservative with time. The distinction with *Salafiyya* is its adherent's belief the *Quran* and *hadith* are the ultimate religious authority in Islam and not the subsequent interpretations or comments by Islamic Scholars.[64] Another distinct characteristic of *Salafiyya* is that it is not a unified movement and is attractive to many Muslims who wish to return to a puritanical form of Islam.

---

[61] Zuhur, 16-17.

[62] Doumato and Metz, 82. These Muslims would like to reinterpret the *Quran* and *sunna* to conform to western standards; namely relating to gender relations, family law, and in some cases participatory democracy.

[63] Christopher M. Blanchard. *The Islamic Traditions of Wahhabism and Salafiyya* (Report for Congress, Washington D.C.: Congressional Research Service, 2008), 2.

[64] Ibid., 3.

Acknowledging that Sunni Wahabbism is the dominant sect in the Kingdom and that its adherents are seen as true Muslims; Shia and non-muslims are often the victims of discrimination and intolerance within Saudi society. This dichotomy is best assessed through the government's treatment of its Shia citizens. The Shia sect of Islam has long been a source of contention within the Kingdom. Again, *Muwahiddun* do not see them as true Muslims, as do many fundamental Sunni sects and their mere presence in the Kingdom are seen as an insult to Islam. The relevance of the Shia in the Kingdom is not that they are seen as the premier internal threat to Kingdom security but as nearly ten percent of the total Saudi population, about 200,000 to 400,000 people within the Kingdom, they have the largest organizational base.[65] The Saudi Shia are constantly viewed through a skeptical lens. This owes in part to their religious affiliation with the country of Iran, which is dominated by believers in the Twelver sect of Shia Islam[66], and is the primary external concern to the Kingdom. This also stems from the 1979 uprisings in which Sunni extremists seize the Grand Mosque in Mecca which leads to Shia in the Eastern province seeking equality in the Kingdom, religiously and economically, to rebel against the government which results in governmental embarrassment as well as violence and instability in the Eastern province of the Kingdom. Both uprisings are quelled but the Shia fare worse than their Sunni contemporaries due to their religious affiliation and Kingdom fear of an Iranian style revolt.[67]

---

[65] Zuhur, 15.

[66] Doumato and Metz, 76, 85. Again, the Shia part from the Sunni in their belief that all rightful religious leadership must be able to trace its lineage back to Imam Ali (through his son Husayn). The Shia in the Kingdom are mostly believers in the sect known as the Twelvers. It is their belief that there were 12 rightful rulers, known as Imams, the last of whom went into hiding in the 9th Century and did not die but will return in time as the *mahdi* (messiah) and create a just and righteous Muslim society. This belief system not only is in contradiction to Sunni beliefs; but, is a direct abomination to Wahabbist beliefs as it is the epitome of *shirk*.

[67] Toby Craig Jones. "Rebellion the Saudi Periphery: Modernity, Marginalization, and the Shi'a Uprising of 1979." *International Journal Middle Eastern Studies* (Cambridge University Press), no. 38 (2006), 215-16.The Saudi's believed the Saudi Shia were influenced by the Ayatollah Khomeni in Iran and were going to stage the same style revolt in the Kingdom. Though inspired by Khomeni he was not their catalyst. Saudi Shia issues remained internal reflected local grievances and objectives not the overthrow of the sitting monarch.

The majority of Shia, 40 percent, live in the Eastern province along the Arabian Gulf. This province maintains the rich oil fields of the Kingdom as well as a strategic geographic location with relation to Iran.[68] Also, the majority of the employees of the oil conglomerate known as the Arabian American Oil Company or ARAMCO are Shia. This unique relationship has many Wahhabis untrusting of Shia intentions. Relations between the government and the Shia have continually become more strained; especially, with the looming threat of Iran to national security. This belief affects Saudi internal security responsibilities between combating deviant threats and securing their Eastern Province from perceived possible Shia insurrection.

In the contemporary Kingdom, the current threats affecting the Kingdom mainly come from extremist Islamic organizations who recruit disenfranchised citizens, mostly youth, utilizing their own brand of Islamic interpretation. According to Sheykh Abd al Aziz Aal Al Sheykh, Grand Mufti of Saudi Arabia, in a *fatwa* he issued on 1 October 2007, "Setting forth to wage jihad without authorization the ruler is a serious transgression…Saudis are being mislead by suspicious elements from the east and the west, who are exploiting them in order to accomplish their own aims…causing serious damage to Saudi Arabia, Islam, and the Muslims".[69] This statement thus establishes official Kingdom stance on those who wish to deviate from approved religious doctrine and set the stage for Saudi response.

Saudi Strategies to Countering Deviants

"…And one who attacketh you, attack him in like manner as he attacked you. Observe your duty to Allah, and know that Allah is with those who ward off (evil)."
The Quran, Surah II, 190[70]

The strategies being implemented by the Kingdom in order to counter the current extremists/terrorists threats are borne out of practical experience. The Saudis make a distinction, as do many of their brother Muslim countries, between dealing with those they consider to be

---

[68] Doumato and Metz, 76 and 85.

[69] Ansary, 124.

[70] Pickthall, 48.

terrorists and those they consider to be extremists or radical moderates. Monte and Princess Palmer, authors of *Islamic Extremism: Causes, Diversity, and Challenges*, best explain the difference in that terrorists or jihadists test the limits of Islamic theology and use acts of terror in order to achieve their ends; whereas, radical moderates or extremists are those who can actually alter their societies through penetrating all reaches of society to include the military and security services. This they do in order to gain credibility for their causes, as did the Muslim Brotherhood in Egypt in the 1970's. They utilize violence as the last resort and offer a state that is seductively modern.[71]

The Saudis are hardly inexperienced at dealing with extremists/terrorists threats to their Kingdom. The first threat to the Kingdom is stifled in the 1920s during the *Ikhwan* Rebellion. In 1979, the Islamist Revolt in Mecca and seizure of the Grand Mosque and Shia uprisings in the East lead to a suppression of Sunni extremists and Shia Saudis that turn the Islamic world on its head.[72] In the 1990's terrorist bombings intensify due to Kingdom involvement in Operation Desert Storm and the stationing of western troops within the Kingdom is seen by some extremists groups as being a "slap in the face" to the *Dar al Islam*, house of Islam or Muslim soil.[73] It is not until the 2003 bombings in Riyadh on Kingdom governmental establishments and widespread terrorist attacks against Muslims in the Kingdom that there is significant action taken by the Saudi government in retaliating against the extremist/terrorist threat.

---

[71] Monte Palmer and Princess Palmer. *Islamic Extremism: Causes, Diversity, and Challenges* (Lanham, Maryland: Rowman and Littlefield Publishers, Inc., 2008), 249.

[72] See Trofimov, 1-7 and 187-197. This revolt was lead by fundamental Sunni elements in the Hijaz at the holy city of Mecca. The Saudi's responded by laying siege to the Kaba and entering with commandos (presumably French led) to retake the holy site and quell the leadership of the revolt. In the East, the Shia chose this as a time to rise up and establish their demand for equality in the Kingdom. This too was put down by troops.

[73] Patai, 14-15. This all relates to how Arabs view their self-image. The Arab nation, *qawm*, the *Dar al Islam* and the *Dar al Harb*, house of war, are the three views Arabs hold of their world; the dilemma being that Arabs see themselves first as a nation of people. Second, Islam or *Dar al Islam* as the inner circle where peace resides and third, the outer circle, being non-Muslim controlled lands or *Dar al Harb*, which are lands where infidels reside and thus subject to conflict because they do not represent Muslim interests.

Many of the Kingdom's critics place the blame on the Saudi security apparatus for failure to act appropriately prior to the attacks of 9/11. The Kingdom has been held accountable by many western officials, i.e. Senator Ron Wyden (D-Ore.)[74], for less than aggressive methods in assisting the global community in countering these threats that many view as home grown. The Kingdom has also been accused of a lack of diligence in attacking Al Qaeda in the 1990's and instead appeasing these organizations, allowing for numerous terrorist attacks in the Kingdom and finally that of 9/11. The Saudi Security Apparatus does not support this view; though they have assumed some responsibility for not being as proactive as their critics would like; for them the effort was in countering not only Al Qaeda but other extremist threats to the Kingdom such as the Egyptian Islamic Jihad and remnants of the Muslim Brotherhood as well as Shiite groups supported by Iran in their Eastern Province.[75] Though this argument has validity, research shows that critics of the Kingdom arguments are just as valid.

The Kingdom's approach to the extremist/terrorist threat is not fully understood by their western allies. Their approach has been less of what we, in the west, understand to be a "hard" or direct approach. The Saudi governments' way of combating these threats is not the conventional approach that those in the west would be most comfortable. The Saudi government initially utilized the hard or direct approach and did not achieve much success in ridding themselves of extremist/terrorist threats to the Kingdom. In fact, what the government quickly came to understand is that the hard/direct approach will only work when you have actionable objectives that are validated being in violation with *Sharia* Law, as defined by the *Ulema*, and definitive enemies of the state. They learn that constantly taking the hard approach leads to the alienation of those who may not necessarily be deviants and in turn lead these moderates to become threats due

---

[74] Josh Meyer. "Saudis Faulted for Funding Terror." *latimes.com.* April 2, 2008. http://articles.latimes.com/2008/apr/02/nation/na-terror2 (accessed October 3, 2008).

[75] Cordesman and Obaid. *Saudi Counter Terrorism Efforts: The Changing Paramilitary and Domestic Security Apparatus*, 4. Cordesman and Obaid have written extensively about the efforts of Saudi Arabia; this article is the most recent and concise read on Saudi security efforts.

to governmental actions. The Saudi quickly uncover, in order to defeat these threats you not only have to take the direct approach but an indirect or "soft" approach when dealing with the flawed or deviated ideology and beliefs of these deviants.[76]

The current governmental approach is what most westerners consider to be asymmetric or unconventional. This approach leads to the development of two strategies which the government believes will achieve their objectives in defeating extremist/terrorist threats within the Kingdom and aide the global community in eliminating these threats. It also offers the global community alternate approaches to countering these threats that may be utilized in their societies.

Each of the strategies is unique in its application and execution; the Saudi government accepts that solely focusing on the elimination of terrorists, rather than on their radical ideology, was misguided and counterproductive[77]. The two strategies they have developed have been best described in an article by Dr. Abdullah F. Ansary, a senior fellow of the Homeland Security Policy Institute at the George Washington University, *Combating Extremism: A Brief Overview of Saudi Arabia's Approach*, He categorizes the hard and soft approaches as the "Security Strategy" and the "Advocacy and Advisory Strategy".[78] These two approaches are the current way forward for the Saudi government in dealing with current and future extremist/terrorist threats.

The Security Strategy: The direct approach to combating deviants

The purpose of the Security Strategy is to conduct direct action measures such as the arrest and/or killing of terrorists and other means, i.e. seizure of assets, to directly affect the ability of extremists/terrorists effective operations as an organization to threaten the Kingdoms internal and external security. This strategy is implemented by all elements of the Saudi security

---

[76] Ansary, 118.

[77] Cordesman and Obaid. *Saudi Counter Terrorism Efforts: The Changing Paramilitary and Domestic Security Apparatus*, 4.

[78] Ansary, 118.

forces and with cooperation of members from the Saudi community.[79] The lead Saudi agency for implementing this strategy is the Ministry of the Interior (MOI) which is led by HRH Prince Nayif, who has been the minister since 1975. MOI is given the responsibility for coordinating all direct action and intelligence gathering of terrorists/extremists within the Kingdom. As such, MOI receives over $8 billion in resources to utilize as Prince Nayif sees fit; his ministry virtually has limitless power when dealing with internal security concerns.

Prince Nayif has long been a pivotal player in maintaining internal security within the Kingdom. His critics believe that he underestimated the Kingdom's security issues and that it is because of his inactions that Al Qaeda and other extremist organizations flourished in the 1990's. His supporters believe him to be the key figure in the Kingdom's war against deviants and give him credit for all Kingdom successes to date, i.e. hundreds of arrests, killing of senior Al Qaeda figures, foiling of bombings within and outside of the Kingdom.[80] Whatever one feels about Prince Nayif the results he and his ministry have achieved are hard to dispute when it comes to successes in the current fight. He alone is given responsibility for modernizing and reorganizing elements of MOI to combat the current threat. It is under his authority that MOI has achieved prominence as the premier anti-terror ministry in the region.

The Saudi Security Apparatus consists of all elements of the Saudi government and armed forces. There are a number of civil ministries that play an indirect role in this strategy; from the Ministry of Finance for their seizure of monetary assets of known terrorists, it was this ministry that froze Osama Bin Laden's assets in 1994, and organizations who support terrorists and extremists to the Ministry of Communication and Ministry of Education conducting their information operations and educational reforms against radical ideologies to the Ministry of Islamic Affairs conducting religious education reform and reeducation of wayward Muslim

---

[79] Ibid.

[80] Cordesman and Obaid. *Saudi Counter Terrorism Efforts: The Changing Paramilitary and Domestic Security Apparatus*, 23.

clergy. All ministries are aligned to support the government it its goal to eliminate threats from the Kingdom and the international community. The U.S. government applauds the Saudi government for its efforts and remains close allies.[81]

In line with the Ministry of Finance the Saudi Arabian Monetary Agency (SAMA), the chief regulatory body for Saudi banks and financial institutions, began implementing an educational program instructing judges and investigators on legal methods to counter terrorist financing and money laundering. In 2004, the Financial Action Task Force (FATF), an international body established by the members o the G-8 countries, concluded that the Kingdom has emplaced financial controls that rival or exceed that of any other country.[82] Opponents of Saudi success in the financial arena state that reliable figures are difficult to obtain due to the fact that relatively small amounts of money required for terrorists go unnoticed; the structure of the Saudi financial system makes financial transfers hard to trace and there are no tax records kept for Saudi citizens; also, charitable contributions, *zakat*, are a religious obligation and are given anonymously and these funds may be diverted from legitimate charities. Usually 2.5 percent of a Muslims wealth is set aside for *zakat*. [83] The Saudis counter this argument in that they established a High Commission for Oversight of Charities in 2003 and the Financial Intelligence Unit in 2005 to counter these issues. However, their findings are not available to the public.

---

[81] Ibid.

[82] Royal Embassy of Saudi Arabia-Information Office. *The Kingdom of Saudi Arabia Initiatives and Actions to Combat Terrorism* (Washington, D.C.: Royal Embassy of Saudi Arabia, 2008), 7. A joint U.S.-Saudi task force on Terrorist Financing operations led to an investigation of 1,098 Saudi bank accounts for suspicious involvement in terrorist financing. Christopher M. Blanchard and Alfred B. Prados. *Saudi Arabia: Terrorist Financing Issues* (Report for Congress, Washington, D.C.: Congressional Research Service, 2007), 23.

[83] Blanchard and Prados, 17. The criticism of *Zakat* is that the donations are not monitored. One expert estimated Saudi charitable donations to be in excess of $3-$4 billion dollars with an estimated 10-20 percent disseminated abroad. Saudi officials have estimated that $100 million in charitable donations are directed abroad each year. These donations help pay for the poor and *madrasas* or religious schools. The biggest problem in tracking donations is that they are usually made by private donors.

The efforts of all governmental agencies are important in this strategy but the critical partner in this strategy is the Saudi security and military forces.[84] The Saudi security forces are a conglomerate of internal security and intelligence services which differentiate from the conventional military forces. Elements of the Saudi Arabian National Guard (SANG), which is an internal security force or Kings Army which operates under direct supervision of the King and is responsible for internal protection of critical Kingdom facilities, serve to provide aid to MOI as does the regular Army which maintains external security responsibility and utilizes its special forces and aviation assets in support of MOI objectives. All these organizations assist in Kingdom efforts in combating terrorists and radical extremist threats.

Again, the lead agency in combating these threats is MOI. MOI contains all the police forces, including the Border and Coast Guard, as well as the internal intelligence organizations one would expect of their western counterparts. The police security forces are responsible for public security and thus fall under the Public Security Administration. The lead unit in this organization in combating Al Qaeda is the Special Emergency Forces. This force acts a rapid response force in the event of an unexpected security threat; they number around 30,000.[85]

Another specialized service is the Special Security Force which is comparable to a Special Weapons Assault Team (SWAT) or the FBIs Hostage Response Team. They are the premier anti-terrorist service of the Kingdom and report directly to Minister of the Interior, though its operational head is HRH Prince Ahmed ibn Abd al Aziz, Assistant Minister for Security Affairs and full brother to Prince Nayif. This force is developed in 1979 after the poor performance of the SANG at the Grand Mosque in Mecca.[86]

The General Security Service (GSS) or *Mabahith*, secret police, are the domestic intelligence service of MOI; this service is the Saudi version of the FBI or Britain's MI-5. It has

---

[84] Cordesman and Obaid. *Saudi Counter Terrorism Efforts: The Changing Paramilitary and Domestic Security Apparatus*, 22.

[85] Ibid., 27.

[86] Ibid.

long been considered the most important and one of the most secretive services in the Kingdom. Prince Mohammed bin Nayif leads this organization and under his leadership the GSS has had success in defeating many plots and continually assists in countering terrorist recruitment. The GSS is extremely well trained and works with foreign police and intelligence agencies to stem the tide of deviant threats. They quickly gained notoriety for being one of the most professional intelligence agencies in the region and their interrogation methods have been credited with thwarting numerous attacks on the Kingdom and abroad.[87] This success has come with a price, many senior officers of the service have become terrorist targets and as such there have been at least 2 attacks on top officials.

The Kingdom's premier foreign intelligence service is the General Intelligence Presidency (GIP). They alone are responsible for foreign security, anti-terrorism, foreign liaison functions, strategic analytical assessments, coordinating foreign covert networks of the Kingdom and ultimately conduct of covert operations on foreign soil if the need arises. The President of the GIP reports directly to the King with an estimated budget of $500 million a year making it the most funded intelligence agency in the Middle East.[88] The President of the GIP is responsible for all intelligence collection and analysis by all intelligence services, MOI/MODA/SANG,in the Kingdom. In reality there is no official Saudi intelligence community. One is currently being formed and as of the writing of this paper may already be in place. The GIP is reported to have a weak research department as are all the intelligence services. The critique is that they all rely too heavily on personal contacts and briefings, rather than systematic and structured intelligence.[89] This is'Arabism', for lack of better term, which needs to be adjusted or reconciled if the GIP is going to be a relevant agency in the future. When all is said and done the Saudi intelligence

---

[87] Ibid., 29.

[88] Ibid.

[89] Ibid., 30.

community will encompass the intelligence services of the Saudi Security Apparatus as well as various ministries' research centers.

One of the most important aspects of security operations to the Kingdom is its Border and Coast Guard.[90] These organizations have long been the Kingdom's first line of defense against all threats and as such there has been a dramatic increase in their capabilities. In the past they mainly dealt with smuggling and infiltration across their borders. Today, it is much the same but with focus being on those who would profit from terrorist activities. It is virtually impossible to secure the Kingdom's borders and coastline; traffic in the Gulf and Red Sea is too high, coasts too long and sensors cannot track all small craft. The land border is too porous and there are not enough Guardsmen to accomplish this task.[91]

This brings us to one of the most controversial organizations within the security apparatus and that is the Committee to Prevent Vice and Promote Virtue, better known as the *Mutawwain* or simply *Mutawwa*, religious police.[92] The *Mutawwa* is an organization unique to the Kingdom, though the Taliban attempt to recreate something similar in Afghanistan in the 1990's. Their primary responsibility is to enforce compliance with Wahhabist doctrine and ensure public observances of religious practices. One can often see them during times of prayer ensuring closure of businesses and ensuring compliance of public dress. Some Saudis see them as an outdated and ultra conservative organization while others see them as a useful group that promotes secularization within the Kingdom. No matter how they are seen they are an integral part of the security apparatus and as such are utilized by the Kingdom's security service.

Finally, the issue of "Saudization" is probably the most direct method which the government currently utilizes to counter internal security threats. The Saudi government has

---

[90] Anthony H Cordesman and Nawaf Obaid. *Saudi Internal Security: A Risk Assessment-Terrorism and the Security Services Challenges and Developments* (Working Draft May 30, 2004, Washington, D.C.: Center for Strategic and International Studies, 2004), 22.

[91] Cordesman and Obaid. *Saudi Counter Terrorism Efforts: The Changing Paramilitary and Domestic Security Apparatus*, 32-33.

[92] Palmer and Palmer, 253.

come to understand that, "emptiness leads to terrorism", and has begun to pour billions of dollars into training young Saudis for professional careers; in 2005 only 13 percent of Saudis filled private sector jobs with the goal being 45 percent.[93] The Saudi government realizes that addressing the economic and educational needs of the people is the best way to counter recruitment of the youth into terrorists' organizations and stem the tide of disenfranchised youth to support the government.

The successes of the Security Strategy are touted by the Saudi government in the numbers of suspects arrested, identified or killed. According to an information paper distributed by the Royal Saudi Embassy Information Office in Washington D.C., the Saudi government acknowledges over 2200 suspects arrested and more than 120 militants killed; 18 of 36 suspects on their Most Wanted list from 2005 have been killed or captured as have 24 of 26 suspects on their Most Wanted list from 2003.[94] In turn the toll on the Saudi Security Apparatus has been high; 90 security officers have been killed and over 200 wounded in this fight.[95]

The Advocacy and Advisory Strategy: The indirect approach to reeducating deviants

Even with all the successes attributed to the Security Strategy the Saudi government has come to the realization that solely focusing on the direct elimination of terrorism is a flawed strategy. They find the direct action approach to be counterproductive, misguided and often leads to terrorist recruitment. The Advocacy and Advisory Strategy complements the Security Strategy by implementing counseling programs and dialogue as well as advisory and advocacy campaigns

---

[93] Cordesman and Obaid. *Saudi Counter Terrorism Efforts: The Changing Paramilitary and Domestic Security Apparatus*, 20.

[94] Royal Embassy of Saudi Arabia-Information Office. *The Kingdom of Saudi Arabia Initiatives and Actions to Combat Terrorism*, 14. See Appendix D.

[95] Ibid.

aimed at combating the word and ideas of extremists and terrorists.[96] The strategy is further

defined by two approaches: Prevention and Treatment. The method of prevention is utilized to

aide in correcting the flawed understanding of *sharia*; whereas, treatment utilizes all methods of

communication available from the internet to dialogue and discussion of ideas with the intent of

convincing extremists that they have deviated from the true path of Islam and the government is

here to guide them back to the true path.[97]

The primary focus of this strategy is to combat thoughts with thoughts and promote

tolerance in accordance with the true values of Islam.[98] The methods the government is

implementing to ensure their success are: a counseling program, tranquility campaign, religious-

authority campaign, media campaign, national solidarity campaign against terrorism,

development of public education, monitoring of preaching, review of sponsored publications,

national-dialogue conventions, control of charities, internet filtering, anti-terrorism legislation and

increased international cooperation.[99] All these programs are monitored by MOI in conjunction

with the Ministry of Islamic Affairs (MIA).

The Counseling Program was founded by HRH Prince Muhammed bin Nayif; it is better

known by its Arabic name, *al Munasahah*. The purpose of this program is to encourage security

prisoners to renounce their radical ideology by psychological and sociological counseling as well

as engaging them in intense religious discussion. It is not a part of the criminal investigation

process.[100] This program is offered mainly to prisoners who have not been involved in acts of

terrorism and is tightly monitored by MOI. It works off of the presumption of benevolence not

vengeance. The Advisory Committee sees the programs subjects as being victims of radicals and

---

[96] Ansary, 118.

[97] Ibid.

[98] Ibid.

[99] Ibid., See article for complete descriptions of all programs.

[100] Christopher Boucek. "Terrorism Monitor." *Jamestown.org* (August 16, 2007) http://www.jamestown.org/terrorism/newsuploads/TM_005_016.pdf (accessed January 12, 2009), 1.

not properly educated in Islamic studies. Most of the subjects became deviants based on extremist books, tapes and most recently the internet. Since its inception in 2004, more than 2,000 prisoners have participated in the program and as many as 700 have renounced their former beliefs and been released.[101] In April of 2007, Dr. Muhammad Al Nujimi, a member of the program, announced that only nine of the 700 released have returned to their previous views.[102] Recently, Dr. Al Nujimi reported of 3200 prisoners subject to the program 1500 have renounced their beliefs and been released.[103] This program does have its detractors who believe that the program is not as successful as reported due to its initial secretive nature and the fact that most prisoners will say anything to be released and therefore they cannot be trusted.

The Tranquility or *Sakinah* Campaign is the Kingdoms internet based project with a focus on refuting extremists' websites, chat rooms and forums to counter the spread of radicalization and recruitment over the internet.[104] This program operates as an independent, nongovernmental organization supported by the government, namely the MIA. Its members are volunteers, both men and women. Its method of operation is to target individuals in chat rooms whom express deviant views then catalogs the dialogue and post it for others to view. Many of these dialogues take place over the course of hours but have been known to last months. The volunteers of this campaign infiltrate known extremists' websites and collect information on their members and also sow dissent within the website amongst its radical members. In 2008, the campaign announced that it had convinced some 877 individuals to renounce their *takfiri* beliefs; those who recant are studied by the research section to determine what approaches are valid.[105]

---

[101] Ibid., 3.

[102] Ansary, 121.

[103] Ibid.

[104] Christopher Boucek "The Sakinah Campaign and Internet Counter-Radicalization in Saudi Arabia" *CTC Sentinel (Combat Terrorism Center)* 1, no. 9 (August 2008), 1.

[105] Ansary,122-123.

Of interesting note, the MIA is sponsoring a growing number of Saudi women preachers seeing as about 60 percent of Al Qaeda sites are known to be operated by women.[106] The success of the campaign is also measured by Al Qaeda attempts to keep followers from engaging with members of the *Sakinah* and also by attempts of Al Qaeda to upload viruses or steal volunteers files.

The Religious Authority Campaign is sponsored by the Council of Senior *Ulema* and is a critical element to countering radical ideology. The main goal of this campaign is to refute illegal *fatwas*, religious decrees. A *fatwa* is declared illegal if it has not been issued with the approval of the *Ulema*. In 2004, the Council issued a *fatwa* condemning acts of terrorism and in 2007, Saudi *mufti*, supreme *Imam*, Sheikh Abd ul Aziz Aal Al Sheikh, issued a fatwa prohibiting Saudi youth from taveling abroad to engage in jihad.[107] The Council recently launched a website that provides information on all *fatwas* authorized by the Council and also acts as another weapon aimed at combating radical ideology.

The National Solidarity Campaign began in 2005 with the aim of gearing the Saudi people as a nation against the ideologies of deviants. This campaign makes extensive use of the media to disseminate the Kingdom's policy against deviance. In 2007, the Ministry of Islamic Affairs initiated a sub-campaign known as the Shielding Campaign, *al Tahseen.*[108]

This program is targeting radicalization through education and ministry. Where this program diverges from others is that it targets youth before they become deviants. This program stimulated the Saudi educational system to reform much of its curriculum and targets those educators who preach intolerance by either dismissing or retraining them. In May of 2007, Saudi public schools carried out an awareness campaign aimed at combating extremism and in February

---

[106] Ibid.

[107] Ibid., 124.

[108] Ibid., 126.

of the same year the Council of Ministers approved a $2.3 billion project to redevelop the Kingdom's public education system.[109]

The MIA is instrumental in conducting a religious monitoring program focused on the reeducation, dismissal or punishment of radical clerics and *Imams*. Since 2003 they have fired over 353 intolerant clergy and suspended another 1367 others.[110] The Ministry conducts electronic monitoring of mosques in Riyadh with the intent that by 2008 all mosques in the Kingdom will be monitored. The MIA has also started to review and redistribute Islamic heritage books and books on contemporary issues.[111]

The common theme throughout these campaigns is the recognition in the utility of negotiation. Negotiations are a cultural and religious norm and obligation. Examples of the importance of negotiation are replete throughout the *Quran* as a tool utilized by the Prophet Muhammad to end conflict, settle disputes or ward off danger from Islamic lands.[112] In his article *Negotiation in Islam*, Professor Wahbah al Zuhaili discusses the religious aspects of negotiation and how they relate to the fundamental resolution of disputes and conflicts in Muslim society. He states, "negotiations are considered of major importance [in Islam] as a positive tool for promoting peace, spreading the spirit of friendship and understanding, improving international relations, and enabling parties concerned to live in security, prosperity and happiness."[113]

The Way Forward?

The questions that remain unanswered are: What relevance do these strategies have in regards to U.S. policy? Is this a way forward for the U.S. in countering these threats? In order to answer these questions effectively, the U.S. must figure out where U.S. and Kingdom policies

---

[109] Ibid, 127.

[110] Ibid.

[111] Ibid.

[112] For further insight see Wahbah Al Zuhaili. "Negotiation in Islam." (*PIN Points*, 2003), 1-4

[113] Ibid., 2.

converge. An argument made by Dr. Ansary is the current Saudi example is the way forward for the United States and her allies. In U.S. Joint Publication 3-0, combating terrorism is defined as, "actions, including antiterrorism (defensive measures taken to reduce vulnerability to terrorist acts) and counterterrorism (offensive measures taken to prevent, deter, and respond to terrorism), taken to oppose terrorism throughout the entire threat spectrum."[114] This definition is interchangeable with combating extremism and outwardly it seems this is what the Saudis have accomplished. According to Dr. Ansary, the British security services have already approached Saudi Islamic theologians to explain *sharia* position on controversial questions and convert extremists in the United Kingdom.[115]

If Dr. Ansary is correct and the British are utilizing Saudi methods this leads one to ask, has the U.S. done the same? Or is U.S. policy so stringent that even though these methods may be a "way forward", the U.S. will refuse to do so out of policy or arrogance? There is no current research to show this to be the case and as for U.S. policy the Bush administration was adamant against any form of negotiation with these groups. The Obama administration speaks of correcting errors of the past administration but it is still too early to tell if their proposed policies will be much different.

This leaves one to conclude that the answers become a matter of opinion. Let us look at the dynamics of the U.S-Saudi relationship. This relationship has a history dating back to the 1930s with the founding of oil in the eastern desert and the establishment of ARAMCO; it is further solidified on 18 February 1943 when President Franklin Roosevelt, in Executive Order 8926, states that the defense of Saudi Arabia is vital to the defense of the United States.[116] With this statement begins an over 60 year commitment from the U.S. to the Kingdom to ensure its

---

[114] U.S. Joint Forces Command. *Joint Publication 3-0: Joint Operations.* Incorporating Change 1, 13 February 2008 (Norfolk, VA: U.S. Joint Forces Command, 2006), GL-8.

[115] Ibid., 130.

[116] Burke, 25

security and stability. Though both countries have had their disputes with one another in the past; both still remain extremely committed to this unique partnership in the region.

The Saudis are the United States' premier Islamic ally in the Middle East and as such the U.S. must remain devoted to this alliance. Furthermore, the Saudis are not only an ally but a major trading partner in the region. [117] The U.S. spends billions in American dollars to aid in the Kingdom's defense and infrastructure; it also, remains committed to Saudi sovereignty and the preservation of the monarchy. It is no surprise that the U.S. is the largest exporter of Saudi oil nor is it a surprise that the U.S. maintains a strategic foothold in the Kingdom coalesced with the maintenance of advisory teams and military sales within the Kingdom. Both countries acknowledge the need for further cooperation in combating terrorism and the understanding is to build upon the successes the Kingdom has made within their current strategy.[118] Bottom line is both profit from this relationship economically and strategically. Also, it is not in the best interest of the U.S. to alienate the unique relationship the Kingdom shares with the Muslim world.

With the interdependence both countries share can the U.S. utilize the same methods as the Saudis? Presently, research does not support U.S. policy. The Bush Doctrine makes it very difficult for the U.S. to gain credibility in the eyes of the Muslim world for being fair and equitable. The Muslim world does not view the policy of preemptive strikes at any government the U.S. sees as a threat as being impartial and equates much of its policy creation on Israeli policy towards the Palestinians.[119] In addition the U.S. is accused of embracing the Israeli list of terrorist organizations as their own and this has created much distrust amongst friendly Muslim nations and organizations such as Hamas, Hezbollah, the Muslim Brotherhood and other

---

[117] Christopher M. Blanchard. *Saudi Arabia: Background and U.S. Relations* (Report for Congress, Washington D.C.: Congressional Research Service, 2008), 33. In 2007, the Kingdom was the largest U.S. trading partner in the region. Saudi exports were estimated at $35.6 billion and imports from the U.S. were estimated at $10.4 billion.

[118] Ibid., 22-23.

[119] Palmer and Palmer, 261. The Bush Doctrine is seen as an anti-Muslim policy in that it represents a lack of concern for civil rights and views terrorists having no human rights and being the ones responsible for the suffering of Muslims not the U.S.

organizations that seek religious reform in that there is no distinction made between terrorists and the radical moderate.[120] Monte and Princess Palmer argue that the U.S. policy not only, "clearly defines war against jihadist but against all Islamic extremism in all of its manisfestations and this is a major break with America's long standig tradition of working with Islamic extremism,"[121] The Palmers also argue that the U.S. need to list their threats in terms of severity and immediacy and must also counter each threat with a suitable strategy posed by the threat. This argument is valid when weighed against the response the U.S. has received from the Muslim community on the GWOT.

When it is all boiled down, the salient point is the willingness to negotiate. The fundamental problem with negotiations is that most if not all western nations refuse to negotiate with terrorist and the fact of the matter is that the west is not the Kingdom. Negotiation is not weakness and this seems to be the prevailing attitude of the West. The United States has stated on many occasions that its policy is not to negotiate with terrorists and in essence this includes the radical extremists who are not terrorists nor have terroristic desires towards the U.S.; the U.S. does not distinguish between the two. With this attitude the United States has already forced its own hand on how it will meet with these threats; directly or not at all. There is no room for negotiation and as such no room for employing certain campaigns utilized in the Advocacy and Advisory Strategy of the Kingdom. For example, the Counseling Campaign involves clear desire to negotiate with the beliefs of radical individuals. Professor Wahbah al Zuhaili, Director of the Department of Islamic Jurisprudence and its Schools, Faculty of Sharia, Damascus University to the Saudi Arabian Foreign Ministry in Riyadh postures that negotiation, as a principle, is taught in Islam as well as Arab culture. He further states, "negotiations are part of the decisive and serious dialogue that takes place between Muslims and others to end conflicts they enable the spread of the Islamic faith, foster good neighborly relations, and strengthen the bonds of

---

[120] Ibid.

[121] Ibid., 262.

cordiality and cooperation or facilitate the conclusion of cultural and economic treaties."[122] This description falls in line with Patai's Arab syndromes of hospitality-generosity and honor-dignity. The Saudis utilize this understanding in their favor and appreciate what negotiation achieves within their socio-cultural norms and mores; this willingness to compromise with deviants gives an edge to the Saudis that the U.S. cannot hope to capitalize upon until they see it the same. Also, given that Saudi *Imams* and clerics as well as the monarchy are seen as the progenitors of fundamental Islam, there is an instant credibility which the west can never hope to duplicate. The Saudis continue to utilize hard and soft methods in their approach to combating deviants in the Kingdom and by doing so achieve what has somehow become elusive to their western allies; a compromise between force and compassion.

Conclusion

The Kingdom was founded on extremist ideology and from this knowledge they have tailored their approaches to the current threat. The Saudis have proven through a combination of both hard and soft approaches that there is an alternative to combating and prosecuting Islamic extremist and terrorist. Their approach is based on practical knowledge of the culture and religion in which terrorist and extremist operate. This understanding places them at a supreme advantage over their western allies. Though, this may be the case, the U.S. should continue to leverage the Kingdom as an example to the region of cooperation between western and eastern ideals. However the U.S. chooses to do this, they must remain aware that this use must stay in line with Islamic cultural norms and exercise patience. In our "fast food" centric society this approach may seem hard to stomach but in the end can be the most beneficial. This does not mean that the U.S. should not continue to support political and social reforms in the Middle East? No, but it must

---

[122] Al Zuhaili, 1.

take care to do so in a manner that does not alienate the region and cause resentment over perceived foreign interference.

The challenge in conducting research on this topic is that there are very few primary resources available on the actual strategies applied by the Saudis. The main sources utilized in researching the Saudi strategy are taken from three secondary sources. One is pro-Saudi, Ansary, and the other two are moderate or favorable to Saudi successes, Cordesman/Obaid and Boucek. Though the Palmers discuss this issue briefly it is not Saudi centric and remains quite vague. With regard to contact made with the Royal Saudi Embassy, the information they provided was cursory and for public consumption. Every attempt at requesting an official definition of what is the Kingdom's definition of an extremist and/or terrorist went unanswered.

Recommendations for further research are to examine the successes of the Counseling and Tranquility campaign. That is, confirm the credits the Saudis give themselves through thorough independent research and analysis. In addition, which of these methods apply to the U.S. and their western allies; Dr. Ansary discusses the British utilizing some of the Saudi methods but leaves to question are these methods translatable to the U.S.? No current research has shown this to be credible. Though these campaigns show promise, they are Islamic centric approaches from a Muslim nation with Islamic bona fides. Further study into U.S. ability to utilize versions of these approaches must be conducted.

In the same respect, further research into Saudi direct action programs requires attention. It is not enough for the Kingdom to claim success through numbers of arrests or kills. Kingdom policies and procedures in the utilization, organization, training, and planning of the forces or units that conduct these operations require future study in order to validate their claims and utility.

Regardless, the Kingdom has remained steadfast in its support to combating extremist and terrorist on the peninsula to the criticism of fellow Islamic states. Though many of their western critics question their sincerity, their methods are sound and show promise in countering these threats. Since 2005, King Abd Allah has sought to strengthen alliances with European and Asian allies as well as maintain steadfast support of U.S. efforts in the region.

Though, when all is said and done the truth of the matter is that the Saudis have something no one in the west will ever have: Instant credibility as Muslims. More importantly as the protectors of two of the holiest sites of Islam and the birthplace of the progenitor of Islam, the Prophet Muhammad. Conservative Islamic states will follow the lead of the Saudis in how they address the issue of deviance and will always support a fellow Muslim country versus a non-Muslim ally; to not do so is an affront to God and no Muslim country would risk the perception of turning on a Muslim brother. In fact Jordan, Syria, Egypt and Lebanon have all taken official stances against terrorists and certain extremists groups, though not all organizations seen as terrorist by the U.S. are seen in the same regard in the Arab world. The Muslim Brotherhood, Hezbollah and Hamas all have a certain degree of credibility as being fundamental Muslim groups that are either seeking freedom from an oppressor or as a radical conservative faction. Does this mean that one cannot be skeptical of their purpose or function? No, it means that in order to gain trust and assistance in this region of the world the U.S. must be willing to seek alternatives to combating the threats of terrorists and extremists. Again, negotiation is a powerful tool that the U.S. needs to analyze, recognize and utilize.

In the end what truly matters is that the threat posed by violent extremists and terrorists is ultimately neutralized if not completely eliminated. In order to aid in this accomplishment alternative measures need to be sought and exercised. The Saudis have shown us alternative methods that show promise and work within the confines of their society.

APPENDIX A-Royal Genealogy

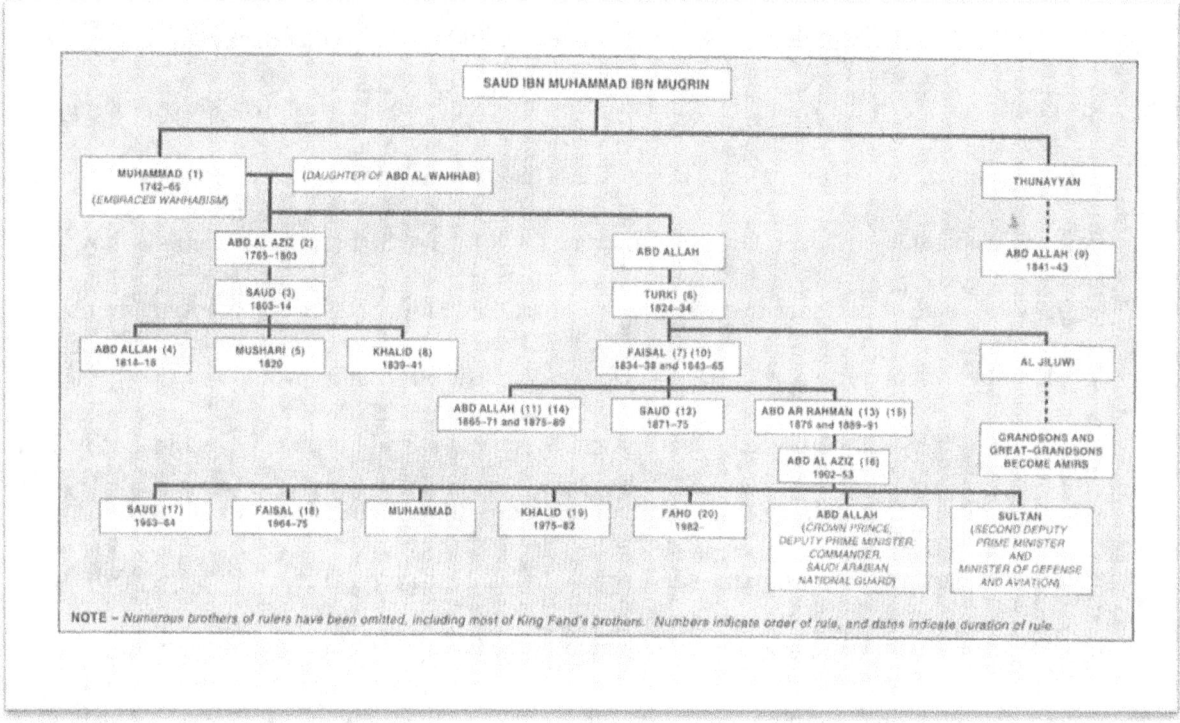

Source: Data from Metz, 22.

Note: This genealogical table represents the House of Saud from the patriarchal begininning to the current house construct of heirs apparent. The current monarch, King Abd Allah, for all intents and purposes became *Malik* in 1996 when Fahd had a stroke which left him incapable to rule effectively. Though not officially named *Malik* (2 August 2005) until the death of Fahd; Abd Allah would be the official face of the Kingdom for nearly nine years with all the rights and privileges afforded the monarch.

APPENDIX B-Glossary

Al Mamlakah al Arabiyah as Suudiyah. Literally the Kingdom of Saudi Arabia.

Al Saud. Literally, the House of Saud; the patrilineal descendants of Muhammad ibn Saud.

Bayaa. The oath of allegiance sworn to those in authority.

Bin. Son of; sometimes referred to as ibn

Bint. Daughter of or refers to a girl or daughter

Caliph. Literally successor to the prophet Muhammad. This title was adopted by leaders of the Muslim community after the Prophet's death.

Fatwa. Religious decree or ruling; an authoritative legal interpretation by a mufti or religious jurist that can provide the basis for court decision or government action.

Hadith. The traditions or the personal acts and sayings of the Prophet.

Ibn. Son of.

Ikhwan. Brother or brotherhood. The zealot Islamic warriors whom Abd al Aziz depended upon to conquer the Kingdom. Their descendants are what is now the Saudi Arabian National Guard.

Imam. Literally 'one who goes before' to lead his fellow Muslims in Prayer. Currently it denotes a religious or spiritual leader. Among Shia the word takes on many complex meanings; in general, and particularly when capitalized indicates that particular descendant of the House of Ali who is believed to have been God's designated repository of the spiritual authority in that line.

Mahdi. The redeemer, though, not mentioned in the Quran; it is believed the Prophet Mohammed foretold of a redeemer who would be sent by God to right society and command a Muslim world. It is believed he cannot be killed by mere mortals, at least not in the first seven years of his reign. Sunni Islam does not believe he has come yet whereas the Shia believe he has come and is waiting to reemerge.

Malik. King

Mutawwiin. Literally, those who volunteer or obey; better known as Muttawa or the Committee for the Propagation of Virtue and Prevention of Vice. Enforcers of Wahhabi norms in public; often called the religious police.

Muwahhidun. Unitarian; this is the literal translation for the movement founded by Muhammad ibn Abd al Wahhab. Commonly referred to as Wahhabis

Quran. Literal translation is 'revelation'. The Muslim Holy Book. Gods revelation to the Prophet Muhammad containing 114 suras or chapters.

Salafi. One who claims to base his understanding and practice on the example of the early generations of Muslims and considers later Muslim tradition a departure from Islam; a term used by Wahhabis and by several other modern revivalist tendencies with varying agendas.

Shahada. Testimony, which explicitly states the central belief of Islam: "There is no god but God and Muhammad is his Prophet".

Sharia. Islamic law.

Shaykh. Literally 'elder' but traditionally connotes tribal leader; contemporary Saudis use it for title for boss.

Shia. A member of the smaller of the two divisions of Islam. Shitte is the singular form. Believe in following the descendents of the Prophet Muhammad's son-in-law Ali, especially the bloodline of his son Hussayn.

Shirk. Polytheism or idolatry, associating creatures with God; a form of unbelief

Sunna. The guide to the proper behavior set forth by the Prophet Muhammad's persona deeds and utterances.

Sunni. The larger of the two divisions of Islam. The believers of this sect rejected Ali's claims and believe they are the true follower of the sunna.

Sura. Refers to chapter in the Quran.

Takfir. To consider somebody and infidel or apostate. Movemetn utilized by Muslims to claim apostacy on other Muslims or claiming non-Muslim behavior.

Taqarub. To accommodate or live in harmony with non-Muslims.

Tawhid. The doctrine of God's unity emphasized by Wahhab.

Ulema. Islamic religious scholars; today the word is utilized for the grouping or council of holy men who regulate religious live in the Kingdom.

Wahhabism. The faith is a puritanical concept of Unitarianism founded by Muhammad ibn Wahhab. Often referred to as Wahhabi or Wahhabis is a name used outside of Saudi Arabia to refer to the adherents of Muhammad ibn Wahhab.

Zakat. Alms giving; traditionally 2.5 percent of ones wealth.

Source: The definitions for the glossary above are taken from the works of Lacey, *The Kingdom*; Metz, *Saudi Arabia: A Country Study*; and Commins, *The Wahhabi Mission and Saudi Arabia*.

APPENDIX D-The Kingdom's Most Wanted

LIST OF 36 WANTED
First published June 28, 2005
Updated April 6, 2007

First: those who are known to have been involved in domestic incidents and are currently at large in the Kingdom:

(1) **Younis Mohammed Ibrahim Alhayari**, a 36-year-old Moroccan who entered the country on a Hajj visa in 1421, then overstayed; he was last known to be hiding with his wife and daughter in the eastern part of the city of Riyadh [killed July 3, 2005]

(2) **Fahd Farraj Mohammed Aljuwair**, a 35-year-old Saudi national who was born in Alzulfi and at one time was living in Riyadh [killed in raid February 27, 2006]

(3) **Zaid Saad Zaid Alsammari**, a 31-year-old Saudi who at one time was living in the area of Alkharj [killed in raid September 4-7, 2005]

(4) **Abdulrahman Salih Abdulrahman Almit'eb**, a 26-year-old Saudi who was born in the area of ALzulfi and is thought to be still resident there [killed December 27, 2005]

(5) **Salih Mansour Mohsin Alfiraidi Alharbi**, a 22-year-old Saudi who at one time was living in the city of Buraydah in Qasim Province [killed in raid September 4-7, 2005]

(6) **Sultan Salih Hosan Alhasri**, a 26-year-old Saudi who at one time was living in Madinah [killed in raid September 4-7, 2005]

(7) **Mohammed Abdulrahman Alsuwailmi**, a 23-year-old Saudi who at one time was living in the city of Riyadh, and was last seen in the area of Alkharj He is skilled in the use of computers and the Internet [killed December 27, 2005]

(8) **Mohammed Salih Mohammed Alghaith**, a 23-year-old Saudi who at one time was living in Riyadh [killed February 24, 2006]

(9) **Abdullah Abdulaziz Ibrahim Altuwaijri**, a 21-year-old Saudi who at one time was living in the city of Buraydah in Qasim Province [killed February 24, 2006]

(10) **Mohammed Saeed Mohammed Alsiyam Alamri**, a 25-year-old Saudi who at one time was living in Madinah [arrested in Madinah July 25, 2005]

(11) **Ibrahim Abdullah Ibrahim Almateer**, a 21-year-old Saudi who was born in Alzulfi, and lived there at one time He was last seen in the area of Alkharj [killed in raid February 27, 2006]

(12) **Waleed Mutlaq Salim Alraddadi**, a 21-year-old Saudi who at one time was living in Madinah; he was last seen in the area of Alkharj [killed in raid April 6, 2007]

(13) **Naif Farhan Jalal Aljihaishi Alshammari**, a 24-year-old Saudi who at one time was living in the area of Hafr-Al-Baten [killed in raid September 4-7, 2005]

(14) **Majed Hamid Abdullah Alhasiri**, a 29-year-old Saudi who at one time was living in Riyadh [killed August 18, 2005]

(15) **Abdullah Mohayya Shalash Alsilaiti Alshammari**, a 24-year-old Saudi who at one time was living in the city of Hail [killed in raid February 27, 2006]

Secondly: those who are known to have been involved in domestic incidents and are presumed to be currently outside the Kingdom:

(16) Noor Mohammed Musa, a 21-year-old Chadian national

(17) Manoor Mohammed Yousef, a 24-year-old Chadian national

(18) Othman Mohammed Hasan Korati, a 23-year-old Chadian national

(19) Mohsen Ayed Fadhel Alfadhli, a 25-year-old Kuwaiti national

(20) Abdullah Wild Mohammed Sayyed, a 37-year-old Mauritanian national

(21) Zaid Hasan Mohammed Hameed, a 34-year-old Yemeni national [reported July 9, 2005 to be under arrest in Yemen]

(22) Fahd Salih Rizqallah Almohayyani, a 24-year-old Saudi

(23) Adnan Abdullah Faris Alamri Alshareef, a 28-year-old Saudi [extradition to the Kingdom confirmed November 8, 2005]

(24) Marzooq Faisal Marzooq Alotaibi, a 32-year-old Saudi

(25) Adel Abdullatif Ibrahim Alsaneea', a 27-year-old Saudi

(26) Mohammed Abdulrahman Mohammed Aldeet, a 21-year-old Saudi

(27) Sultan Sinaitan Mohammed Aldeet, a 24-year-old Saudi

(28) Salih Saeed Albitaih Alghamdi, a 40-year-old Saudi

(29) Fayez Ibrahim Omer Ayyoub, a 30-year-old Saudi [surrendered July 1, 2005]

(30) Khalid Mohammed Abbas Alharbi, a 29-year-old Saudi

(31) Mohammed Othman Mufreh Alzahrani, a 44-year-old Saudi

(32) Abdullah Mohammed Salih Alramyan, a 27-year-old Saudi

(33) Mohammed Salih Sulaiman Alrushoodi, a 24-year-old Saudi

(34) Saad Mohammed Mubarak Aljubairi Alshihri, a 31-year-old Saudi

(35) Ali Mater Ibrahim Alosaimi, a 23-year-old Saudi

(36) Faris Abdullah Salim Aldhahiri Alharbi, a 22-year-old Saudi

Source: http://www.saudiembassy.net/documents/most-wanted-list-June2005.pdf

Note: The Most Wanted List is the Saudi answer to finding those they deem responsible for terror activities within the Kingdom.

Bibliography

Aarts, Paul, and Gerd Nonneman. *Saudi Arabia in the Balance: Political Economy, Society, Foreign Affairs.* New York: New York University Press, 2005.

Abdullah bin Abdulaziz, King. "Royal Embassy of Saudi Arabia: Issue-War on Terrorism." *Royal Embassy of Saudi Arabia.* May 13, 2003. http://www.saudiembassy.net/Issues/Terrorism/IssuesTer.asp (accessed January 12, 2009).

Abu Khalil, As'ad. *The Battle for Saudi Arabia: Royalty, Fundamentalism, and Global Power.* New York: Seven Stories, 2004.

Al Zuhaili, Wahbah. "Negotiation in Islam." *PIN Points*, 2003: 1-12.

Al-Rasheed, Madawi. *Contesting the Saudi State: Islamic voices from a new generation.* New York: Cambridge University Press, 2007.

Ansary, Abdullah F. "Combating Extremism: A Brief Overviewf Saudi Arabia's Approach." *Middle East Policy* XV, no. 2 (Summer 2008): 111-142.

Arab News. *Arab News.com.* http://www.arabnews.com/ (accessed October 3, 2008).

Blanchard, Christopher M., and Alfred B. Prados. *Saudi Arabia: Terrorist Financing Issues.* Report for Congress, Washington D.C.: Congressional Research Service, 2007.

Blanchard, Christopher M. *Saudi Arabia: Background and U.S. Relations.* Report for Congress, Washington D.C.: Congressional Research Service, 2008.

Blanchard, Christopher M. *The Islamic Traditions of Wahhabism and Salafiyya.* Report for Congress, Washington D.C.: Congressional Research Service, 2008.

Blanchard, Christopher M., and Alfred B. Prados. *Saudi Arabia: Terrorist Financing Issues.* Report for Congress, Washington, D.C.: Congressional Research Service, 2007.

Boucek, Christopher. "Terrorism Monitor." *Jamestown.org.* August 16, 2007. http://www.jamestown.org/terrorism/newsuploads/TM_005_016.pdf (accessed January 12, 2009).

Boucek, Christopher. "The Sakinah Campaign and Internet Counter-Radicalization in Saudi Arabia." *CTC Sentinel* (Combat Terrorism Center) 1, no. 9 (August 2008): 1-4.

Bradley, John R. *Saudi Arabia Exposed: Inside a Kingdom in Crisis.* New York: Palgrave Macmillan, 2005.

Brigadier General Al-Mufarih, Ahmed S. *The Role of the Kingdom of Saudi Arabia in Combating Terrorism.* Strategy Research Project, Carlisle: U.S. Army War College, 2004.

Brigadier General Malik, S.K. *The Quranic Concept of War.* First Indian Reprint. New Delhi: Himalayan Books, 1986.

Burke, David M. *Saudi Security: Challenges for the Post-Saddam Era.* Master Thesis, Monterey: Naval Postgraduate School, 2004.

Commins, David Dean. *The Wahhabi Mission and Saudi Arabia.* London; New York: I.B. Tauris, 2006.

Cordesman, Anthony H. *Saudi Arabia: Friend or Foe in the War on Terror?* Testimony to the Senate Committee on the Judiciary, Washington D.C.: Center for Strategic and International Studies, 2005.

Cordesman, Anthony H., and Nawaf Obaid. *Al-Qaeda in Saudi Arabia: Asymmetric Threats and Islamist Extremists.* Working Draft: Revised January 26, 2005, Washington, D.C.: Center for Strategic and International Studies, 2005.

Cordesman, Anthony H., and Nawaf Obaid. *Saudi Counter Terrorism Efforts: The Changing Paramilitary and Domestic Security Apparatus.* Washington, D.C.: Center for Strategic and International Studies, 2005.

Cordesman, Anthony H., and Obaid Nawaf. *Saudi Internal Security: A Risk Assessment-Terrorism and the Security Services Challenges and Developments.* Working Draft May 30, 2004, Washington, D.C.: Center for Strategic and International Studies, 2004.

Cordesman, Anthony, and Nawaf Obaid. *Saudi Militants in Iraq: Assesment and Kingdom's Response.* Monograph, Washington, D.C.: Center for Strategic adn International Studies, 2005.

Coughlin, Con. *Saudi Arabia Can Rein in Taliban and Al Qaeda-Telegraph.co.uk.* March 10, 2008. http://www.telegraph.co.uk/opinion/main.jhtml?xml=/opinion/2008/10/03/do0304.xml (accessed October 3, 2008).

Council on Foreign Relations. *Update on the Global Campaign Against Terrorist Financing.* Second Report of an Independent Task Force on Terrorist Financing, New York: Council on Foreign Relations, Inc, 2004.

Countrywatch. "Saudi Arabia-2008 Country Review." *countrywatch.com.* 200. http://www.countrywatch.com/saudi arabia (accessed October 2, 2008).

Doumato, Eleanor Abdella, and Gregory Starrett. *Teaching Islam: Textbooks and Religion in the Middle East.* Boulder: Lynne Rienner Publishers, 2007.

Erlikh, Hagel. *Saudi Arabia and Ethiopia: Islam, Christanity, and Politics entwined.* Boulder: Lynne Rienner Publishers, 2007.

Federal Research Division-Library of Congress. *Country Profile: Saudi Arabia.* Country
Profile, Washington D.C.: Library of Congress, 2006.

Hanley, Charles J. *Saudi Arabia: Royal Family Gets Quiet Help From U.S. Firm With
Connections.* March 22, 1997. http://www.corpwatch.org/article.php?id=11176
(accessed February 11, 2008).

Important.ca. *Five Pillars of Islam.* 2005. http://www.important.ca/five_pillars_of_islam.html
(accessed December 13, 2008).

Jones, Toby Craig. "Rebellion the Saudi Periphery: Modernity, Marginalization, and the Shi'a
Uprising of 1979." *International Journal Middle Eastern Studies* (Cambridge
University Press), no. 38 (2006): 213-233.

Kingdom of Saudi Arabia Ministry of Islamic Affairs. *Al-Islam.* October 2, 2008.
http://www.al-islam.com/eng/ (accessed October 2, 2008).

Lacey, Robert. *The Kingdom.* First American Edition 1982. New York: Harcourt Brace
Jovanovich, Publishers, 1981.

Lewis, Bernard. *The Crisis of Islam: Holy War and Unholy Terror.* New York: Modern Library,
2003.

Menoret, Pascal. *The Saudi Enigma: A History.* NewYork: Zed Books, 2005.

Meyer, Josh. "Saudis Faulted for Funding Terror." *latimes.com.* April 2, 2008.
http://articles.latimes.com/2008/apr/02/nation/na-terror2 (accessed October 3, 2008).

Niblock, Tim. *Saudi Arabia: Power, Legitimacy, and Survival.* London; New York: Routledge,
2006.

Oren, Michael B. *Power, Faith, and Fantasy: America in the Middle East, 1776 to the present.*
New York: W.W. Norton, 2007.

Palmer, Monte, and Princess Palmer. *Islamic Extremism: Causes, Diversity, and Challenges.*
Lanham, Maryland: Rowman and Littlefield Publishers, Inc., 2008.

Patai, Raphael. *The Arab Mind.* Revised 1983 edition. New York: Hatherleigh Press, 2002.

Peterson, John. *Saudi Arabia and the Illlusion of Security.* London: Oxford University Press for
the International Institute for Strategic Studies, 2002.

Pickthall, Marmaduke William, trans. *The Koran.* Ninth Printing. New York: Alfred A. Knopf,
1992.

Royal Embassy of Saudi Arabia-Information Office. *The Kingdom of Saudi Arabia Initiatives
and Actions to Combat Terrorism.* Washington, D.C.: Royal Embassy of Saudi Arabia,
2008.

Smyth, William, Eleanor Abdella Doumato, Fareed Mohamedi, Eric Hooglund, and Jean R. Tartter. *Saudi Arabia: A Country Study.* Fifth Edition. Edited by Helen Chapin Metz. Washington, D.C.: Library of Congress, 1993.

Sorenson, David S. *An Introduction to the modern Middle East.* Boulder: Westview Press, 2008.

Trofimov, Yaroslav. *The Siege of Mecca: The Forgotten Uprising in Islam's Holiest Shrine and the Birth of Al Qaeda.* New York: Doubleday, 2007.

U.S. Joint Forces Command. *Joint Publication 3-0: Joint Operations.* Incorporating Change 1, 13 February 2008. Norfolk, VA: U.S. Joint Forces Command, 2006.

Zuhur, Sherifa. *Saudi Arabia: Islamic Threat, Political Reform and the Global War on Terror.* SSI Monograph, Carlisle: Strategic Studies Institute, U.S. Army War College, 2005.

www.ingramcontent.com/pod-product-compliance
Lightning Source LLC
Chambersburg PA
CBHW080552290526

45790CB00006B/2631